Privacy-Preserving AI Models in Cloud-Based Cybersecurity

AF668181

ABOUT THE AUTHOR

Amit Goswami is an industry leading thinker and inventor in Cloud, Cyber security and AI with over 6 years of experience in the IT industry. Amit Goswami holds a master's degree in Computer Information Systems from Calums University. Currently, he is a Senior Software Engineer at Source Infotech Inc. and engaged with Humana client. He has worked to develop new techniques for improving privacy and security in the cloud. He has led many large scales Cloud, Cyber Security and AI migration and implementations for businesses to harness the power of clouds.

Throughout his working years, he wrote several great articles and research publications related to Cloud Computing, Cyber Security, and AI. In addition to that, Amit Goswami has spent a considerable amount of his career designing advanced security architectures for organizations to counteract modern day cyber threats in the cloud era. Amit Goswami has also participated in other cutting-edge research projects to advance the state of cloud security.

He has served as a Judge in Cognitive Science during the California Science and Engineering Fair. He has also attended various conferences, including the World Research Forum for Engineers and Researchers, IEEE, where he presented and reviewed research papers in various journals. He published the UK Design Pattern and the India Software Pattern as well.

CONTENTS

List of Figures

List of Tables

CHAPTER 1

Privacy-Preserving AI

1.1 Overview

This chapter explains how Artificial Intelligence (AI) has impacted on many sectors by maintaining the array of processes, refining decisions, and boosting performance. In cybersecurity, we have realized that artificial intelligence can act as a strategic differentiator to combat latter kinds of threats in real time.

According to Ansari et al. (2022), there is the impact of AI on cybersecurity whereby AI is used to boost machine learning that can help look at large databases to infer potential threats and develop the system's robustness. AI forms part of the cybersecurity measures and is used at three levels: detection level, vulnerability level, response to the events level, and predictive level (Camacho, 2024).

Cybersecurity frameworks that include AI have helped firms improve the pace of risk identification, minimize repetition of certain procedures, and lower response times. Kaur et al. (2023) note that due to this characteristic, AI has enhanced security within enterprises, and sharpened its defences' visibility. For instance, AI can detect such attacks as advanced persistent threats (APTs) and ransomware attacks that the traditional system misses (Folorunso et al., 2024). Such a shift is particularly noteworthy today given the fact that the modern world is characterized by renamed cyber threats.

1.2 Challenges

One can consider that the usage of cloud services as the key form of the delivery of computing resources has produced various novelties in regard to the data security and privacy. In the cloud environments, one is likely to store or process large volumes of consumable and valuable data across multiple systems, making the system prone to intrusions, data leaks, and violation of consumers' rights to privacy (Folorunso et al., 2024).

Furthermore, outsourcing carrier operations to third parties creates valid questions about the compliance of the data with legal acts that regulate the protection of personal data such as GDPR and HIPAA. Latest cases like the one where Barings Law sued Google and Microsoft bear ample testimony to the fact that public wants justice where its data and/or privacy rights have been compromised.

These companies have been accused of eavesdropping on users for the purpose of training artificial intelligence languages with private information, emails, etc. as alleged by Poireault, (2025). They provide lessons to encourage the development of privacy-preserving AI technologies that enhance accountability of data controllers.

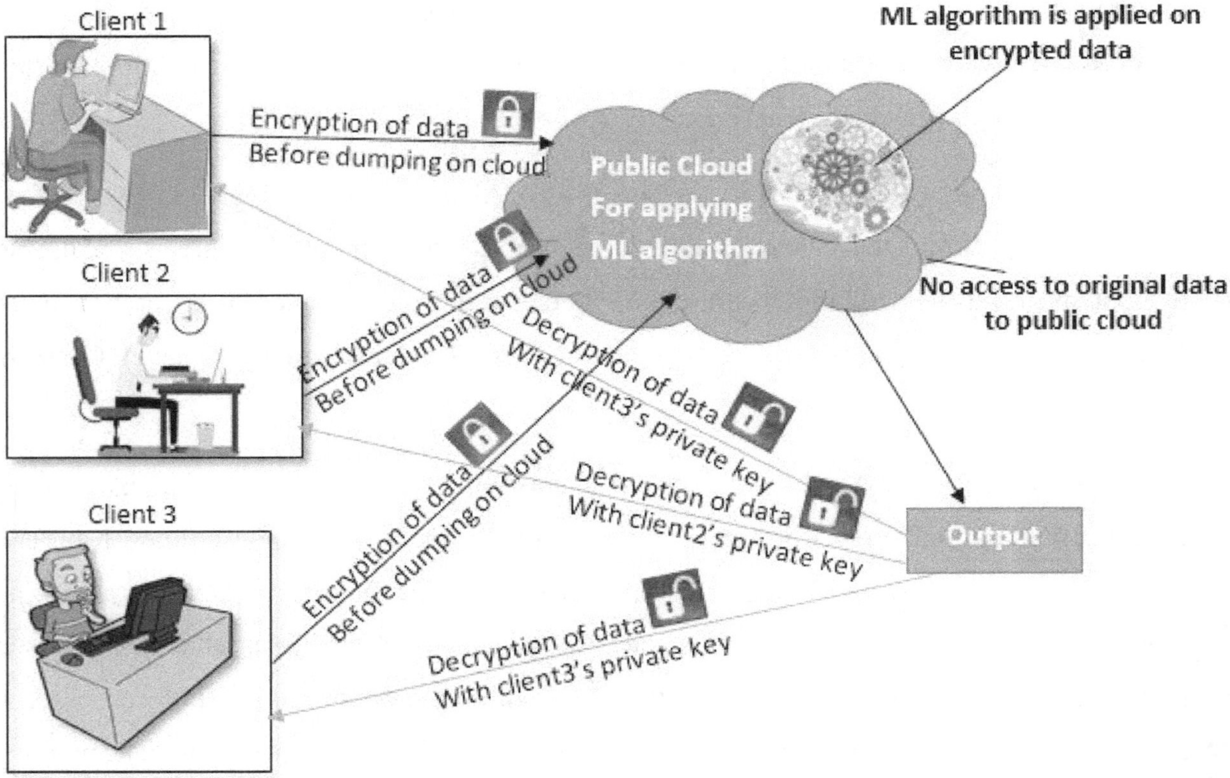

Figure 1 Privacy-Preserving AI Model (Analytics Vidhya, 2022)

One of the threats is the new approach to penetrate a system – adversarial AI – where one AI controls the other AI to attack a certain system or manipulate a certain data set. For instance, Coker (2025) observes that malicious actors launching image-based malware and generative AI, will penetrate email security mechanisms. As these novel and emerging attack vectors are thought to be more capable of evading traditional detection, greater protection and privacy solutions are required in AI and cloud platforms.

1.3 Privacy-Preserving Techniques

Privacy protection measures are crucial to establishing the secure growth of AI applications in the cloud infrastructure. Such methods are federated learning, differential privacy, and homomorphic encryption, all of which are designed to learn data without exposing data. According to Camacho (2024), Twitter needs to strike a balance between automation using AI and attendant ethical and privacy issues for the tool to go mainstream.

1.4 Applications

- **Threat Detection:** AI is also proficient at distinguish new types of malwares, ransomware, and phishing because of various deviances from the normal patterns of behavior of a network. Kaur, Gabrijelčič, and Klobučar (2023) highlighted that the application of the real time understanding of cyber threats, the algorithms of the ML can predict and mitigate the likelihood of the cyber threats happening.
- **Automated Incident Response:** AI led solutions have reduced the time in trying to address those breaches. According to Camacho (2024), the four states of playing fake defence with cyber threats include the use of AI in identifying infected systems, reducing the impacts of cyber threats and regaining balance for a moment.
- **Fraud Detection:** AI is especially irreplaceable when it comes to fraudulent works, for example, unauthorized credit card transactions. According to Folorunso et al in their paper pending 2024, they argue that ''more complex AI models continue to be trained to address emerging threats. AI is still important in compliance and regulatory Framing and testing.

Table 1 AI Applications

AI Application	Description	Privacy Challenge	References
Threat Detection	Finds outliers in data	Potential misuse of user data	Camacho (2024); Kaur et al. (2023)
Predictive Analytics	Looks forward to cyber threats and attacks	Unclear procedures of the decisions made by the use of artificial intelligence	Folorunso et al. (2024)
Security Compliance	Implements or supervises compliances with business	Use of compliance operational reports by	Folorunso et al. (2024)

	or civil regulatory legal codes	other people other than the target group	
GenAI in Malware	Add viruses to image files	It avoids using ordinary security protocols such as firewalls.	Coker (2025)
AI Model Training	Fosters its algorithm development with use of big data	Unauthorized data collection	Poireault (2025)

Those privacy-preserving methods are helpful in mitigate ethical concern and improving cybersecurity. Some of the techniques include; Federated learning for example, enables AI systems to be trained from multiple sources of data without having to access them directly which will compromise the user's privacy (Michael et al., 2023).

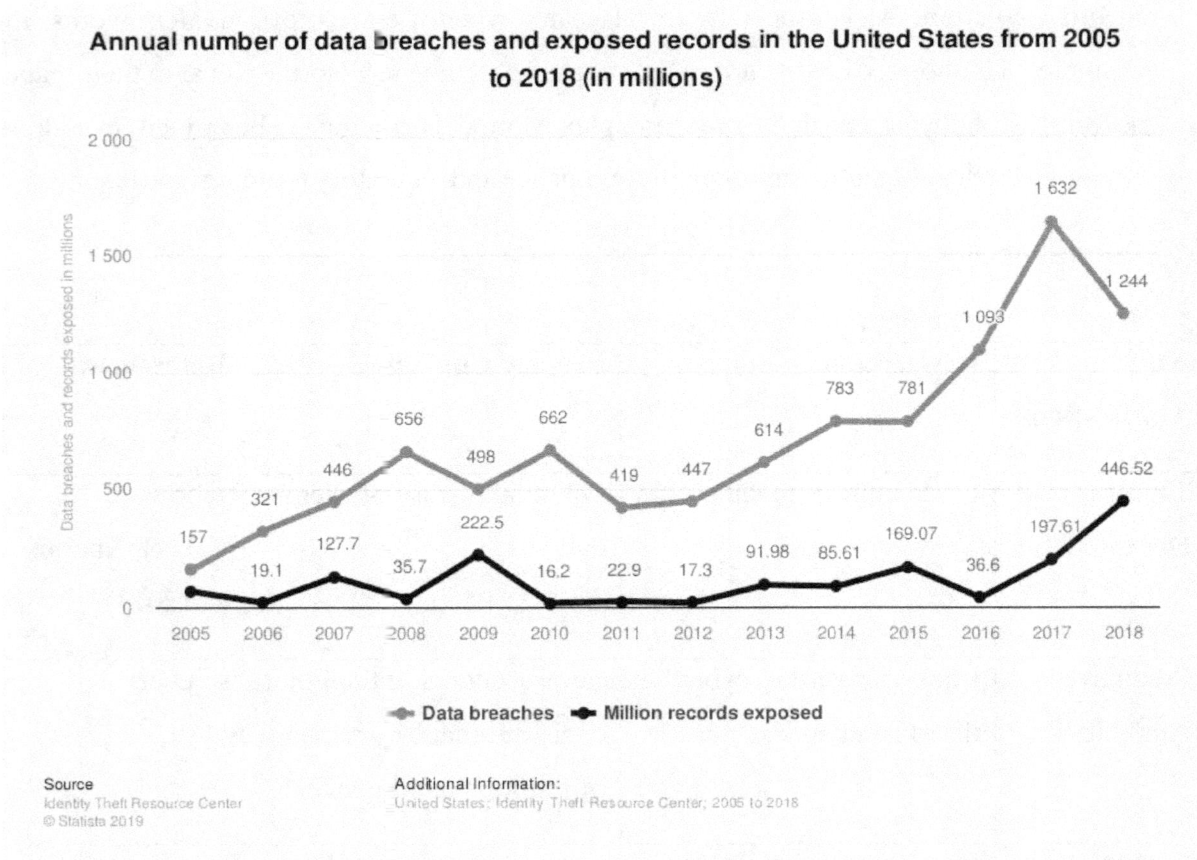

Figure 2 Pirvacy-Preserving records statistics (Fast Forward Labs, 2019)

Differential privacy puts noise in dataset so that even if the data is possessed by an adversarial party, it cannot be easily utilized for further analysis while the dataset still remains useful for further analysis.

1.5 Cloud Security

There has been a rapid growth in the development of cloud computing, lots of organizations such as Microsoft are now pumping billions of dollars into cloud computing expansion to support AI workloads (Cisco, 2025). This growth has led the emergence of possibilities for businesses to embrace AI capabilities leading to concern of data privacy and compliance.

One policy change is allowing sign-ups with anonymous numbers from the Fragment blockchain marketplace which Telegram pioneered, which has shown the potential of improving users' anonymity (Owen-Jackson, 2024). But as much as these advancements offer solutions in their various fields, they also create new risks as criminals among society will find these platforms as fertile ground for their illicit business.

Therefore, among the best practices that the cloud security for the future may be recommended there can be encryption techniques, multi-factor authentication, and monitoring. There should therefore be increased use of AI in driving these systems since they ensure that there is a minimal level of human interjection. Folorunso et al., (2024) expound on how AI can help simplify the monitoring of compliance to given compliance frameworks such as PCI-DSS.

1.6 Limitations

Still, like any innovative technology, AI in cybersecurity is not beyond the drawback. The key limitation is the continued absence of high-quality data as the core value for driving activity. Similarly, in the study by Ansari et al. (2022), it resulted that when a wrong or partial set of data is collected, then wrong threat scores are obtained, which could mean a wrong positive or a wrong negative or the exact opposite.

Adversaries, for instance, have also begun using AI systems themselves, hacking AI with adversarial machine learning. Michael, Abbas, and Roussos (2023) term this as the AI paradox featuring how the same technology that is used to protect systems can also be used by the cyber attackers.

In addition, the cost associated with the implementation of artificial intelligence systems is rather high especially to firms or companies with a low capital base. Folorunso et al. (2024) also posited that currently, organizations have not done sufficient work in expertise to implement and manage AI-based cybersecurity frameworks successfully. Thus, there is a digital gap, and smaller companies become more exposed to threats.

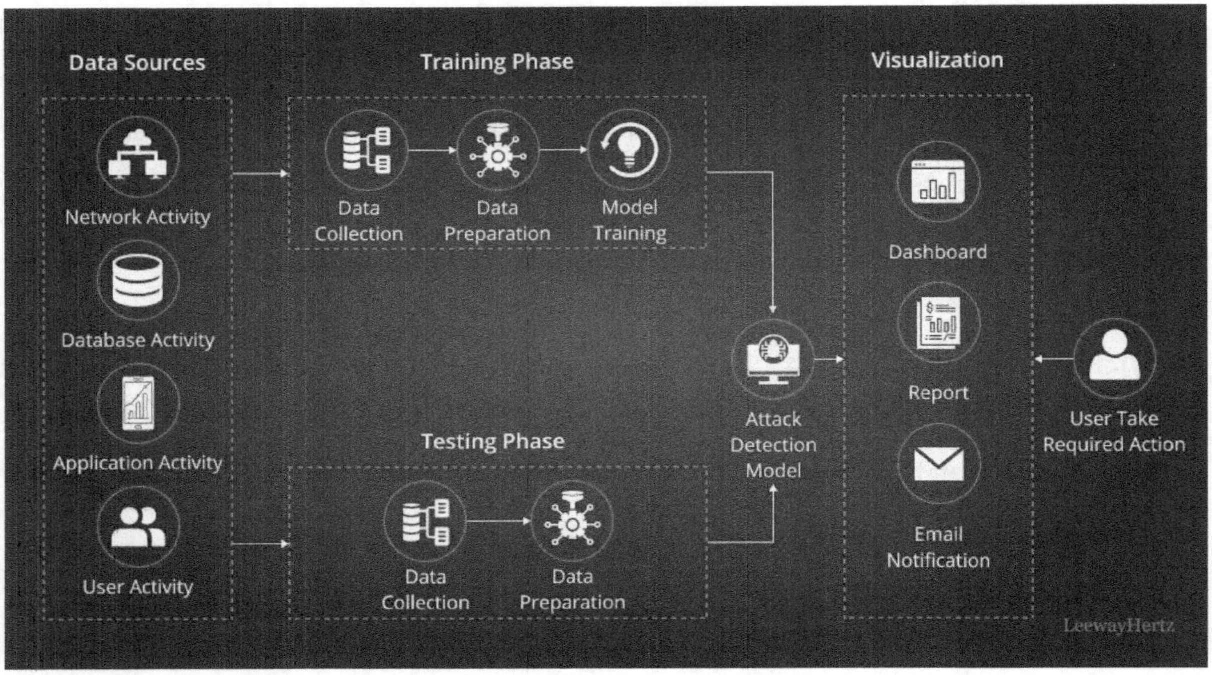

Figure 3 Data security in AI (LeewayHertz, n.d.)

1.7 Conclusion

When it comes to the combination of artificial intelligence and cloud security, one must admit that the processes of protection of the organization's network and the data contained in it from various cyber threats combined with the concern for the privacy of data can be easily transformed into a brand-new level thanks to both technologies.

However, this is also important to have its complexity, such as the ethical issue, adversarial AI, and the regulation also is an issue. Major applications of AI in days to come include federated learning, differential privacy, and homomorphic encryption to enhance reliability.

If these challenges are met, this innovation will help organizations to adopt AI solutions in the cybersecurity sphere and improve risk protection, as well as increasing trust among clients, partners, and employees. The trend of AI in cybersecurity can be seen as issues of artificial intelligence adaptation in cybersecurity related to modern values and existing legal norms, meaning the balance between technological progress and human rights and freedoms.

CHAPTER 2

Homomorphic Encryption

2.1 Overview

Homomorphic encryption (HE) has been described and developed as a revolutionary cryptographic solution for overcoming some of the mainstream weaknesses and risks of encryption for protecting data confidentiality during their processing. Cryptography as described by Acar et al (2018) in traditional models of encryption and decryption involves sharing of a private key or a public key.

While such systems afford a basic level of protection in terms of confidentiality these solutions leave encrypted data vulnerable to privacy concerns especially where these are implemented by third party actors like cloud solution providers (Asante et al., 2021). Before processing can take place with these kinds of data, the data has to be deciphered and this leads to more problems.

This is where homomorphic encryption steps in and discourages the need for data to be decrypted in order for computations to be made by allowing computations to be made directly on said data without necessarily decrypting it. This feature is particularly useful in cloud computing where service provision entails openness to the internet which raises privacy issues.

Homomorphic encryption has been provider of one of the essential parameters to define and develop the modern paradigms of data security. Privacy-preserving computation has been defined for decades, but until Craig Gentry's work on Fully Homomorphic Encryption (FHE) in 2009, FHE has been theoretically applicable (Acar et al., 2018).

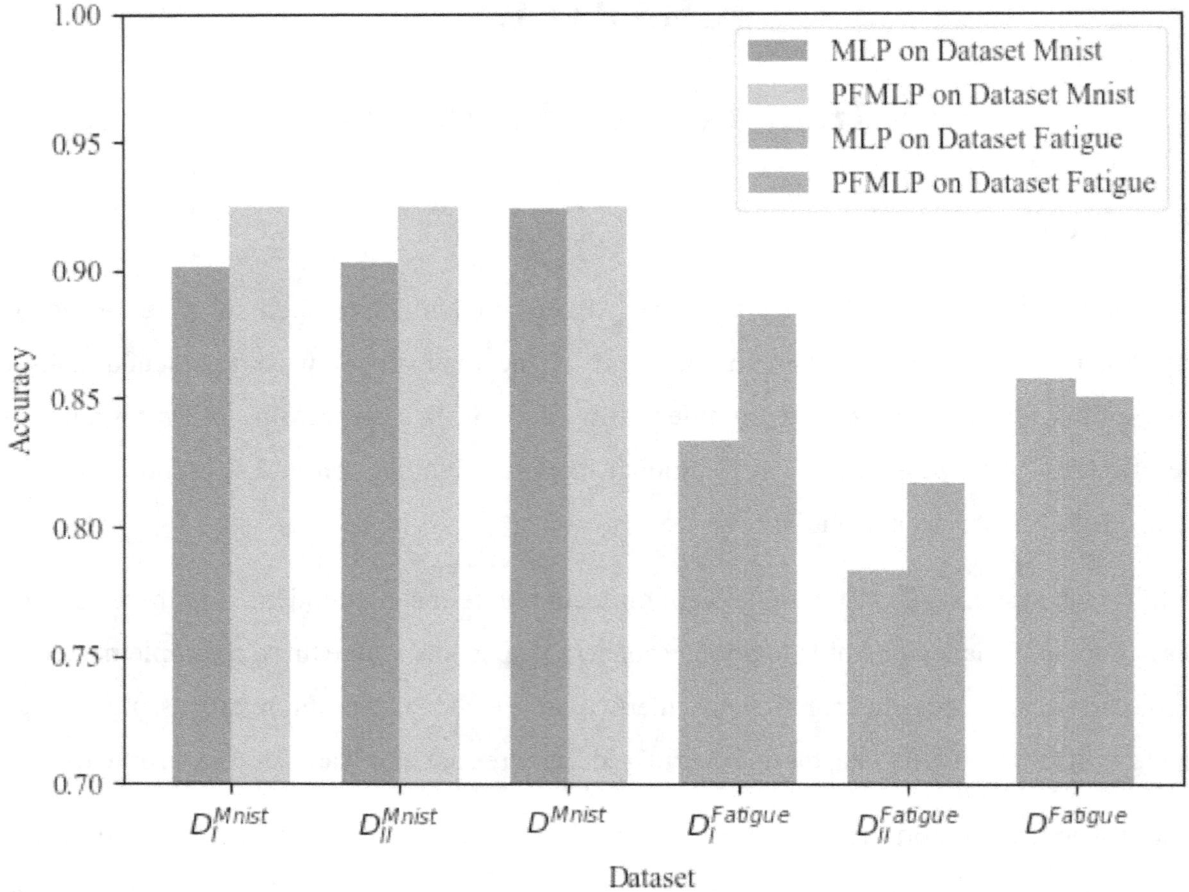

Figure 4 Homomorphic Encryption with Federated Learning (MDPI, 2021)

This work of Gentry made FHE to come up to prove that it is capable to perform any computation on the encrypted data and this has been marked a big achievement in cryptography. However, Acar et al. also notes that despite the fact that the theoretical consequences of FHE are vast, practical applications of FHE have suffered from certain difficulties, specifically, computation complexity and extensibility.

These limitations have encouraged much effort in the development of partial homomorphic encryption (PHE) and somewhat homomorphic encryption (SWHE) as intermediate goals to FHE. While most of these schemes are mathematically simple and relatively incapable of large computations, they form the ground floor on which modern FHE systems are built from.

Munjal and Bhatia (2023) argue that the application of homomorphic encryption in certain forms of applications, including healthcare, where data security is crucial, can bring the desired changes. There are few applications, which should be secured like patient health records since they contain a great amount of personally identifiable information that should be protected against leakage. The old ways of protecting data can only be processed after passing through a decryption phase such that data is vulnerable to breaches.

This issue is solved by homomorphic encryption which allows computations on encrypted data, and only the encrypted data are available to service providers. This capability not only improves the privacy of data but also enables a broader compliance with stringent regulation in data protection making homomorphic encryption a valuable tool for industries that heavily depend on data processing.

The general consequences of homomorphic encryption are also traceable in the further advancement of PETs. As pointed out by Koerner (2023), FHE is a fundamental building block in the still-evolving space of PETs along with numerous techniques like differential privacy and federated learning.

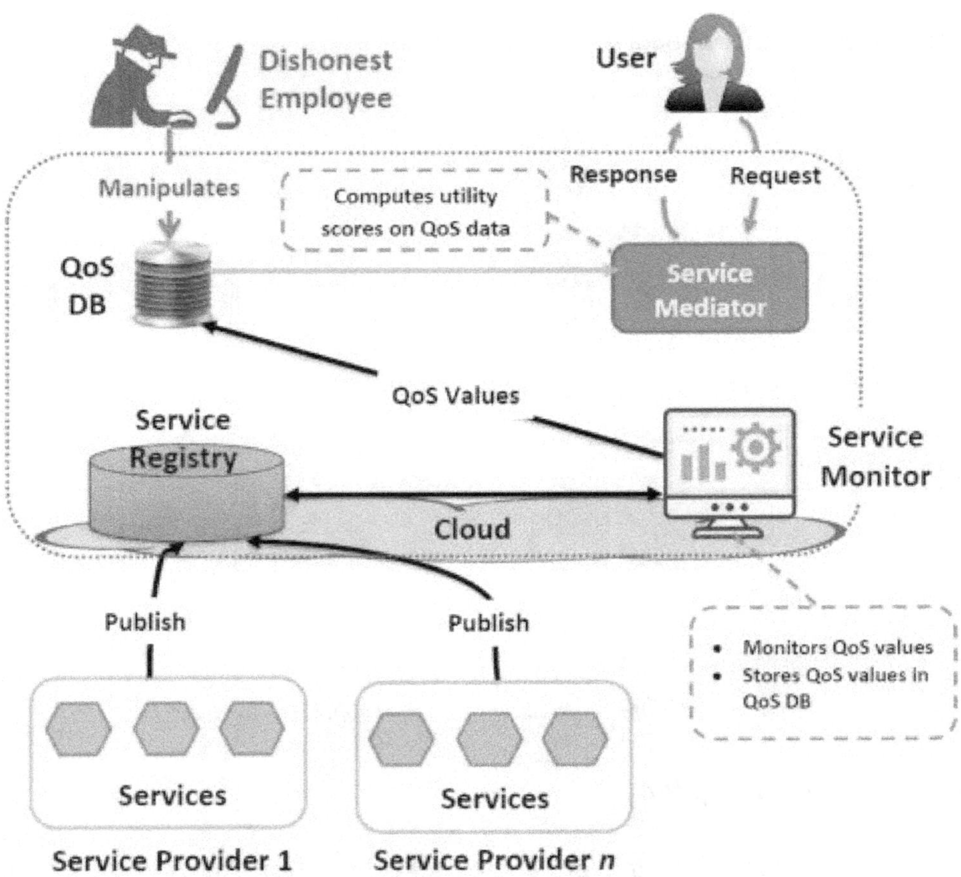

Figure 5 Privacy Preserving services through Homomorphic Encryption (ScienceDirect.com, 2019)

Collectively these technologies sign a revolution in privacy, which has necessitated the creation of data sharing and analysis environment without trading off personal privacy. The latest developments in FHE have been demonstrated by Vaultree, which Businesswire (2024) focused on, as a practical example of the further development of this field.

This next-generation FHE algorithm from the company solves long-standing pains regarding performance and scalability of homomorphic encryption and expands practical use of homomorphic encryption in many fields. Through the use of FHE in all its innovations, Vaultree shows that the transformative technology enables secure data sharing, encrypted machine learning, and adherence to data protection standards worldwide.

Homomorphic encryption can be seen as a revolutionary improvement in the field of cryptography as being able to combat the key problems that are linked to conventional encryption approaches as well as common encryption systems. Starting from the theoretical definition and ending with its specific implementations in various fields – including the healthcare sector and cloud computing, HE brings unprecedented opportunities to protect data and perform valuable computations at the same time. Over the years, with more technological advancements in the field of research more organizations will tap into homomorphic encryption and it will transform the face of data security/protocol.

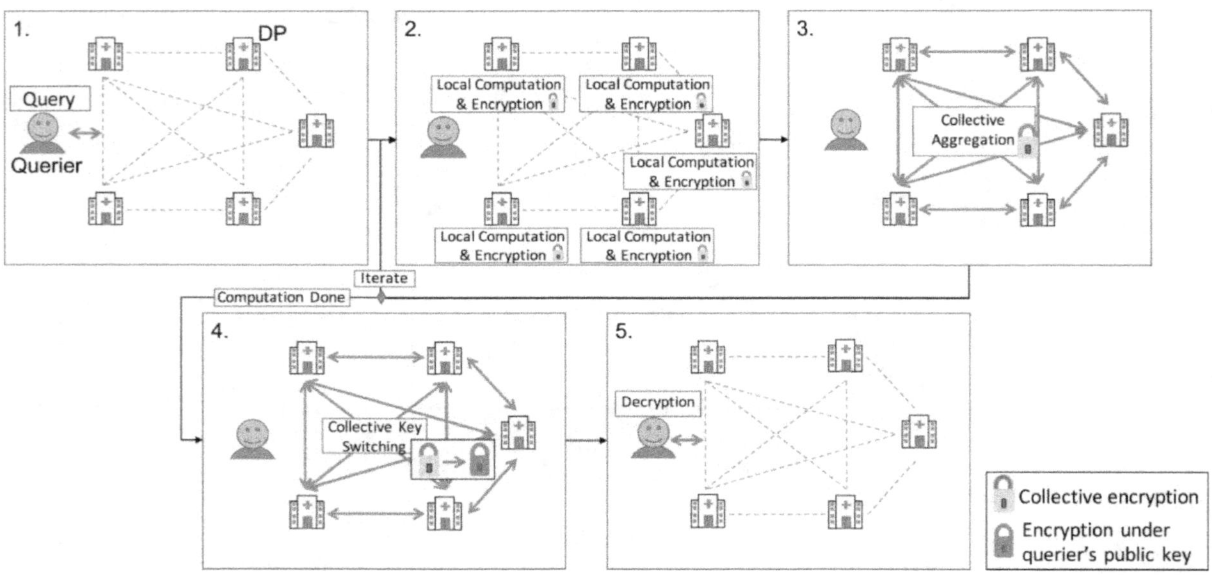

Figure 6 Multiparty Homomorphic Encryption (Nature, 2021)

2.2 Privacy through Encryption

Both homomorphic encryption and privacy-preserving computing are strategically used to safeguard data when undergoing computations and also to facilitate privacy constraints in multi-party and collaborative environments. The above technologies apply to various needs that companies face today such as, privacy leakage, data breaches, and adherence to set regulations.

Several privacy-preservation approaches, including the federated learning models, have illustrated remarkable progress. For example, Huang et al. (2022) came up with an asynchronous federated learning privacy-preserving computing model referred to as AFLPC suitable for the 5G-V2X context.

This model uses zones with adaptive communication protocols that provide personal differential data shuffling to handle noise as well as other problems like single points of failure and parameter aggregation. The experiments showed that the proposed AFLPC keeps its credibility and privacy in FL scenarios. Despite the need to integrate homomorphic encryption and PP methods is still important in secure data exchange in IoV as well as other sensitive applications.

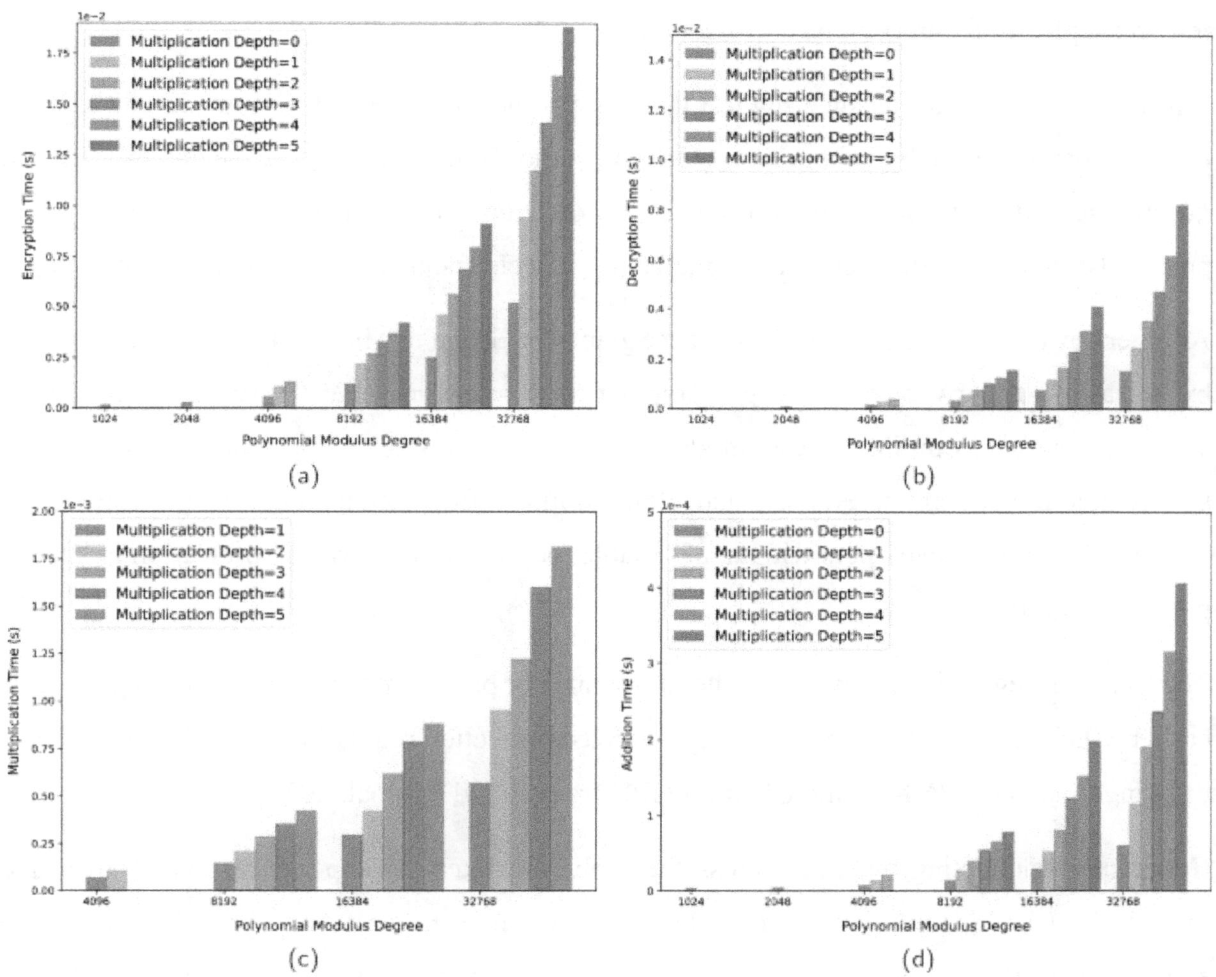

Figure 7 Federated Learning Privacy-Preserving (Cybersecurity SpringerOpen, 2024)

Apart from Federated Learning, privacy-preserving computations are now acknowledged widely to require PETs. In their recent work, Domingo-Ferrer and Blanco-Justicia (2020) offer a detailed discussion of PETs and the areas of private communications, privacy-preserving computation, and database management, to which PETs are relevant.

These technologies are therefore consistent with data protection strategies of design which include hiding, control and enforcement thereby facilitating privacy by design in organizations. Thus, technologies that can be applied to process data securely in untrusted environment include Trusted Execution Environments (TEEs), Computing on Encrypted Data (COED) methods, and Statistical Disclosure Control (SDC) technologies (Global, 2021).

It permits organisations to meet data protection legislation including GDPR and HIPAA besides compromising efficiency. Smart computing techniques or privacy-preserving computing technologies (PPCTs) become more important in today's world of multiple parties' integration, moving applications, and mobile crowdsourcing.

Bashir et al. (2024) for instance suggest that there is increasing need for protection of identity, data and location in such environments. Altogether, the findings of the narrative review raise the question regarding the path towards both better protection of personal data and utilization of the potential derived from development of smart and connected devices and distributed computing.

Another key actor in this space is the Chinese giant Ant Group that has also made a big step here by releasing its privacy-preserving Computation Framework (BW Businessworld, 2022). This framework combines these modern security technologies like Secure Multi-Party Computation, Differential Privacy, and Homomorphic Encryption into a single framework which will provide developers with an affordable tool to improve privacy protection in several party data sharing.

The trends in regulations only add to the importance of privacy-preserving computing, as seen earlier. GDPR is just one of the many standardized protection regulations with the same level of stringency as CCPA from the US and LGPD from Brazil (Global, 2021).

Companies conducting business across the globe are likely to experience lots of legal and management issues, and two or more legal systems may prove to be contradictory. It also encourages health professionals to carry out several analyses, which reduces these challenges through the use of PPCTs to analyze and share data without revealing raw data.

According to Gartner, the adoption of privacy enhancing computation technique is expected to increase to at least 60 percent among large organizations to incorporate in analytics, business intelligence and cloud computing by 2025s (Global, 2021; BW Businessworld, 2022). That deliverable trend underlines that privacy-preserving computing is a transformative paradigm to enable solutions for novel security and privacy threats in the digital era.

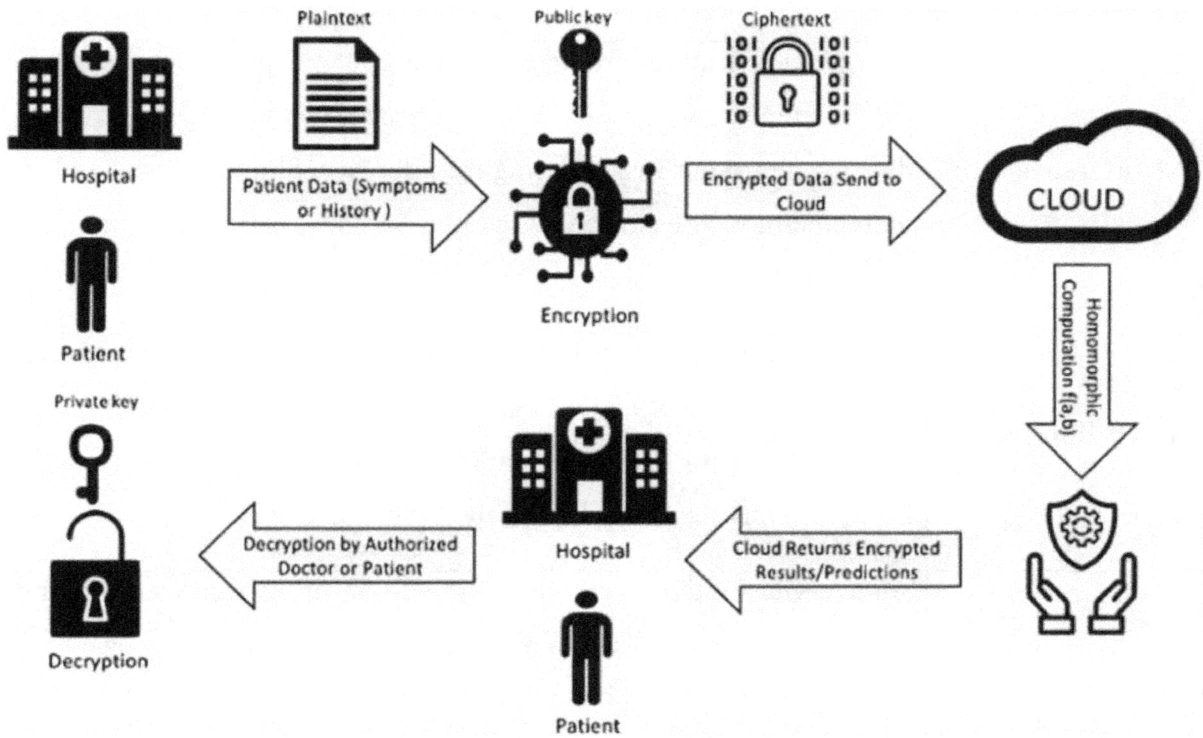

Figure 8 Homomorphic Encryption in healthcare (ResearchGate, 2023)

Technologies for homomorphic encryption and privacy-preserving computing are indispensable when organizations and individuals are aiming at protecting data privacy, following regulations, and collaborating in a connected world. Through the use of federated learning, PETs and PPCTs, any organization can overcome intricate issues associated with data security and privacy across numerous applications including the IoV and multi-party data sharing. Proceeding with investment and developments in this area, will hold the key to tackling the continually changing features of the economics of data.

2.3 Applications in AI

Table 2 AI model training applications

Application Area	Description

End-to-End Encryption (E2EE)	The implementation of AI models in E2EE systems cause a number of issues for security and legalities. It is also proposed to declare technical design principles and user consent options for compatibility with E2EE security (Knodel et al., 2024).
AI Inference	The two new features presented to enhance the AI inference security are “Inference Privacy (IP)” which guarantees that the users’ private data is safe from invasion during the inference. Some are input and output perturbations to achieve a trade-off between privacy and function (Tian & Tandon, 2024).
AI Training	The protection of the data privacy using homomorphic encryption HE to work on the encrypted data and trains the artificial intelligent model. Shown for integrating data from plural origins, helping small hospitals enhance AI models safely (Ang, 2024).
Blockchain	An overview of the decentralized framework of the federated learning process on the blockchain to train models while maintaining data anonymity. Homomorphic encryption allows sharing gradients securely, and especially in medical image classification, such as COVID-19 (Kumar et al., 2022).
Cryptography	Implementation of Responsible AI systems which integrate cryptography in order to overcome issues of privacy. Homomorphic encryption allows computations on encrypted data; privacy persistence through the AI processes (Lauter, 2022).
AI-Assisted E2EE	Looking into the opportunity to evaluate AI application as the part of E2EE systems with the focus on secure communication and conflict between AI and confidentiality (Knodel et al., 2024).
Privacy Guarantees for AI Models	Patterns for preserving the confidentiality of the user’s input during artificial intelligence decision-making distinct from LDP to expose novel performance and adversarial considerations (Tian & Tandon, 2024).

2.4 Encryption in cybersecurity

- Homomorphic Encryption enables performance of computations on encrypted data; that provides security and confidentiality in various areas including the health sector and the financial domain. (Mollakuqe et al., 2024).
- Traditional machine learning eliminates the need to decrypt data that has been, say, collected, and the presence of such data in the process of analysis is likely to be leaked in the event of a breach in security (Dumbere & Ambhaikar, 2020).
- In practice, it may cover the encrypted control of industrial motors where homomorphic encryption can be implemented in real-time for detecting cyber-attacks for instance signal and parameter falsification.
- Secure control messages adapted employed control system by using a keyed homomorphic public key encryption scheme for operations and attacks detection.
- Computer systems in homomorphic environments are capable of implementing computations to the encrypted data while at the same time guarding the privacy of the data, in contrast with non-mutability issue inherent in most conventional cryptographic systems.
- Over the last few years, optimizing some algorithms and parameters like quantizers have brought down the overall computation time and its involvement in errors hence making the encrypted control systems better suited for live operations (Miyamoto et al., 2023).
- Real-world use includes usage in cloud-security application, secure data sharing and threat detection system, therefore enhancing the scalability and privacy.
- The performance and practical applicability of homomorphic encryption is shown through comparison with actual results from simulated healthcare and financial data.
- The results of case studies and expert interviews presented strategies and outcomes of homomorphic encryption system adoption and the corresponding practical concerns.
- In the literature review, a comparison of one homomorphic encryption to another reveals their effectiveness for various applications and which areas of could benefit from some algorithmic enhancement.

- Due to its capability to allow safe outsourcing of computations and include and anonymise conditions into data analyses comprehensively, homomorphic encryption is altering data safeguard and personalization protection processes in a connected global environment (Mollakuqe et al., 2024).

CHAPTER 3

Differential Privacy

3.1 Foundations and Principles

Differential privacy is established as a well-accepted primitive in data security and privacy preservation and provides mathematical assurance of individual data from large datasets while still allowing meaningful analysis. This has been anchored on the principle of the kite that Nobody's data point should make a big difference in any analysis when included or excluded from the dataset.

This guarantee, represented by a quality known as epsilon (ε), guarantees that adversary cannot know with high probability if an individual data was in the dataset; hence robust privacy. Due to this, differential privacy is unique and important in regard to contemporary problems that exist when organizations and governments are releasing sensitive datasets; for example, large scale censuses.

For example, the governments used the differential privacy to make sure that even when people's statistics are revealed, their individual identity will be protected and they substantiate how useful it is for the balance of privacy and utility (Zhang, 2024).

The loose mathematical structures carrying the formulation of differential privacy are critical to its applicability. When integrated into data queries as calibrated noise, it guarantees that the results of these queries are statistically sound without infringing an individual record's confidentiality. which identifies an important requirement of today's advanced data analysis: the information must remain invulnerable from opponents, but at the same time provide collective conclusions.

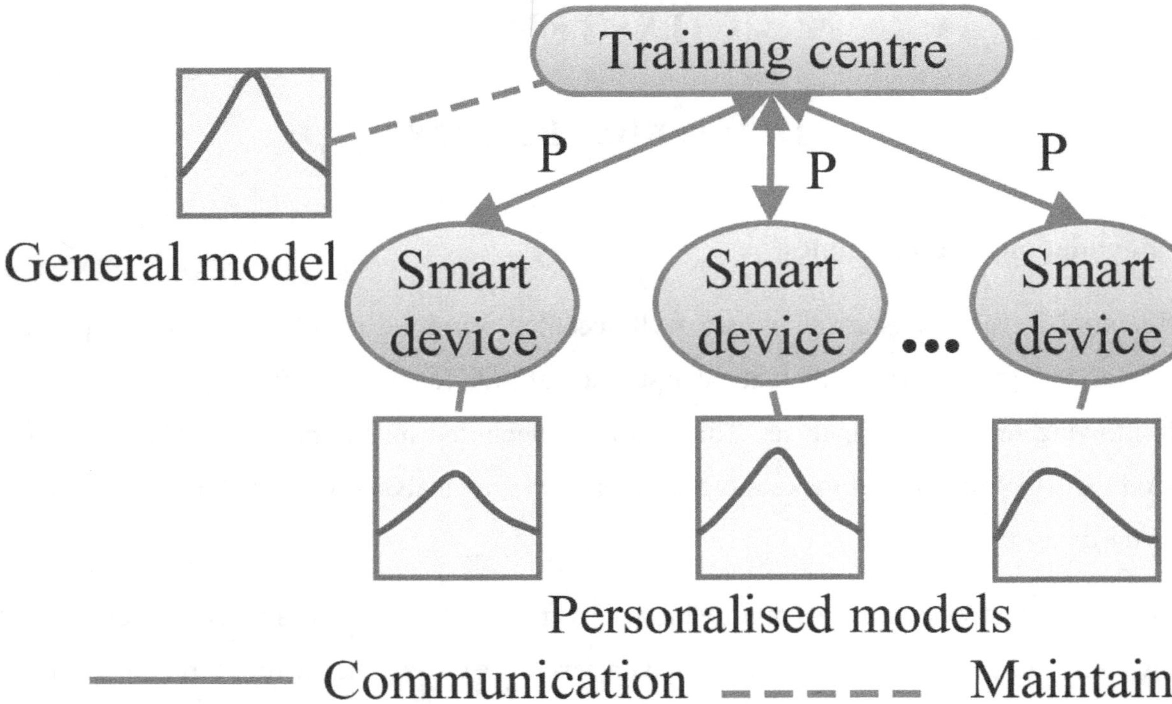

Figure 9 Differential Privacy in AI (IEEE Computer Society, 2022)

This is especially the case given the integration of differential privacy in other sophisticated mechanisms such as dynamic consent management systems. Khalid et al. (2023) used the example to show how differential privacy, when taken together with the other techniques including blockchain and zero-knowledge proofs, offers enhanced security in the context of dynamic consent models.

These systems, which is becoming critical for sectors like e-healthcare, has highlighted how differential privacy can well serve sectors that need to adhere to high levels of regulation as GDPR and at the same time provide secure and privacy preserving data sharing.

However, differential privacy does not only preserve privacy; it also serves other fields including cybersecurity and AI. In the cybersecurity field, differential privacy can prevent inevitable attacks by an enemy and evaluate the true price of a leak, which will complement the enhancement of the cybersecurity system.

Zhang (2024) discusses how, for example, game-theoretic models combined with differential privacy make it possible to overcome some challenges that were once considered nearly impossible to solve, including protecting against adversarial manipulations and secure information sharing in essential systems.

Likewise in AI, differential privacy makes it possible to build fairer and more stable models while at the same time, making it impossible to exploit sensitive data. Of the use cases, Zhu et al. (2020) take cognizance of its application in distributed machine learning as well as deep learning frameworks because of preservation of privacy in subsequent systems.

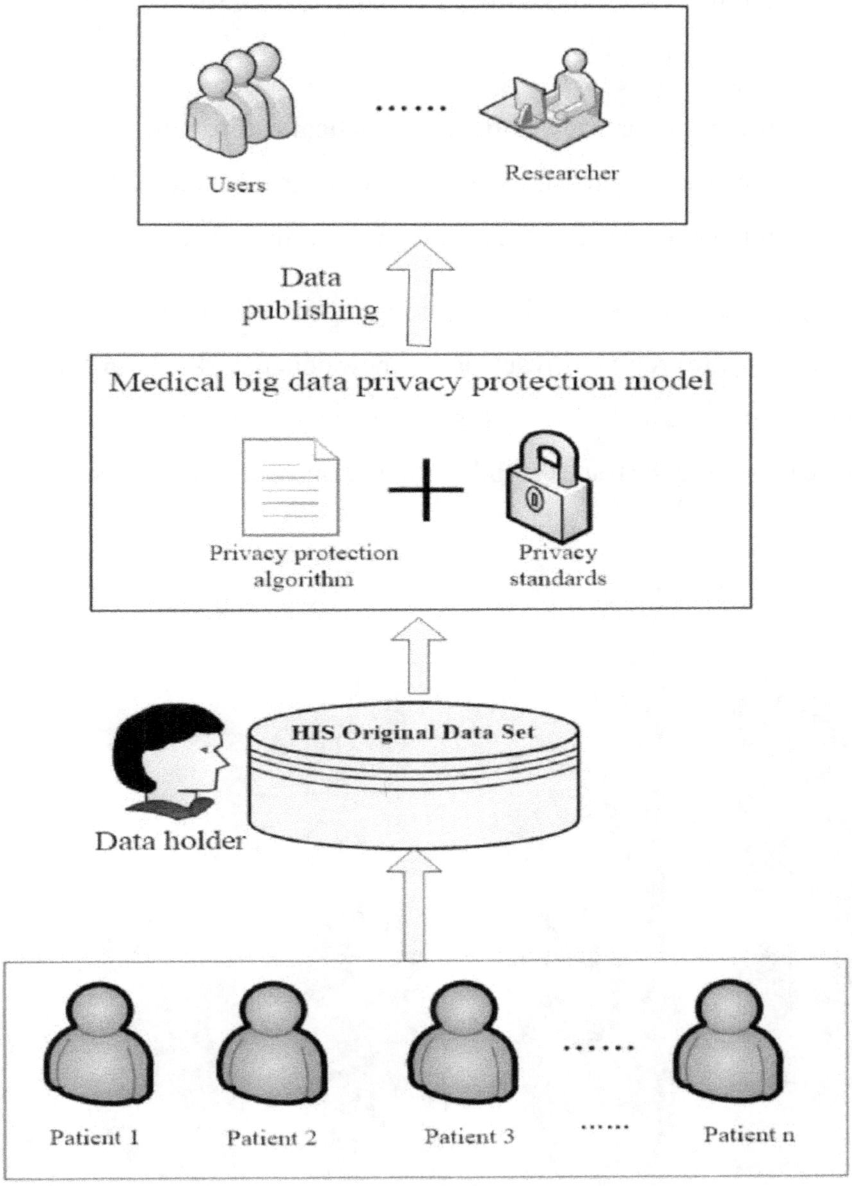

Figure 10 Differential Privacy in medical data (Nature, 2022)

This has shifted the emphasis more toward privacy-preserving technologies, and it is led by differential privacy. Gopireddy (2023) pointed out that it becomes increasingly paramount to combine differential privacy with other powerful technologies including homomorphic encryption, federated learning, etc., so as to deploy systems that are secure, yet operational.

Such integration not only improves privacy but also guarantees that such systems will continue to be sufficiently flexible to address the modern security threats that are characterized by their constant evolution. In light of utility and privacy, differential privacy becomes extremely useful in preserving confidentiality in sensitive data while simultaneously ensuring the credibility in analytical results and thus, it becomes a fundamental approach to data protection in the present-day operations.

Thus, the basis of differential privacy is the mathematical theorem that underpins it; offering the best assurance of privacy. Its use cases span across various domains from secure census data sharing to AI and cyber security transforms its potential.

In achieving secure data dissemination, locking down learning models, and eliminating adversarial subversion, differential privacy has set new benchmarks towards the safety of data in a connected world. Due to its ability to integrate future technologies, it plays and will continue to play a critical role in solving the issues of today's data centric environments.

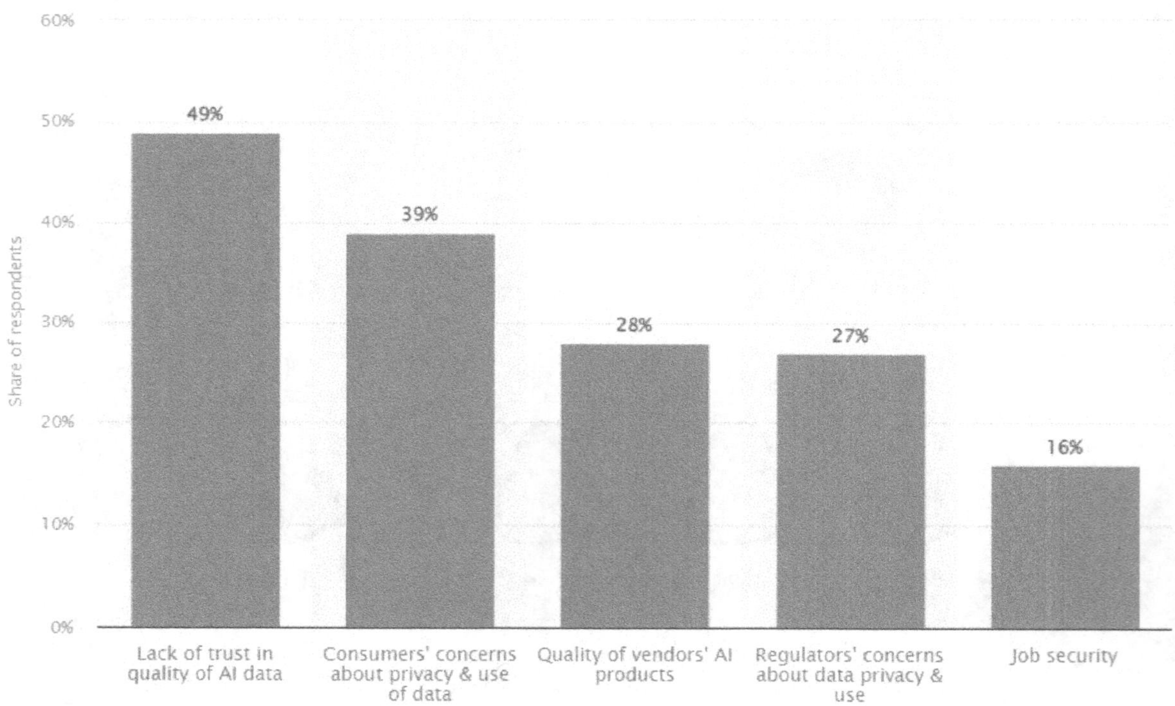

Figure 11 Trust issues in AI (Statista, 2019)

3.2 Techniques

Differential privacy occurs through different approaches to prevent the leakage of sensitive data in data analysis. There are three fundamental ways to perform differential privacy –

Laplace noise addition, Gaussian noise and randomized response. Laplace noise addition entails adding noise derived from Laplace distribution, adjusted for the query sensitivity and the privacy budget (ε).

This technique is optimum for numerical type of questions where sensitivity can be quantified with reasonable accuracy. Gaussian noise addition, however introduces noise which is selected from Gaussian distribution, and is used typically in stronger privacy preservation requirements or in cases where the privacy loss needs to be spread across more queries.

Randomized response techniques are also generally applied in survey data collection; it enables the respondent to respond to the sensitive question honestly, and the answer contains some element of randomness to discourage the identification of the particular response in question. These mechanisms are fundamental to differential privacy due to the fact that they allow the results to remain meaningful statistically while not including anyone's information within that dataset.

Privacy budgets (ε) are one of the most essential components of deploying the differential privacy technique. It specifies how much data can be used in exchange for knowing the privacy of that data. Specifically, the lower values of ε give users stronger privacy assurance, but they harm the usability of the data due to higher levels of noise.

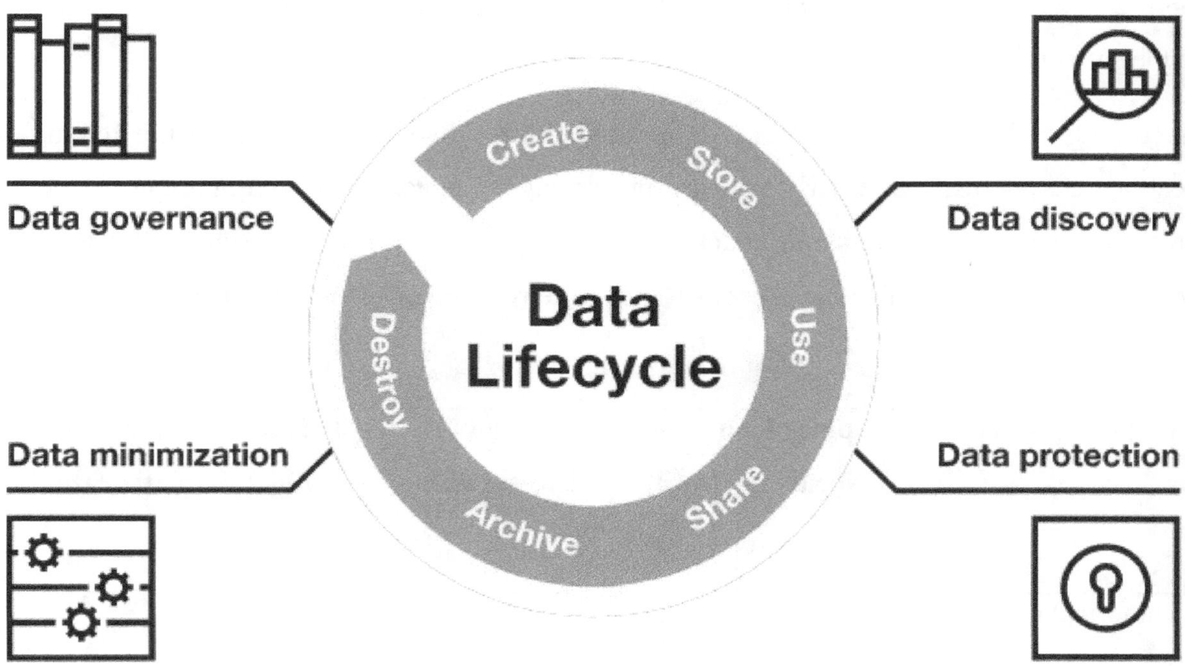

Figure 12 Data lifecycle (Harvard Business Review, 2021)

On the other hand, higher ε values increase utility but they decrease the levels of privacy protection. Authorization limits can be flexible and dynamic; therefore, authorizing multiple queries on the same data will not take the privacy budget to the limit. This dynamic allocation is especially important in real time systems where continuous ad-hoc queries are made on a stream of data.

For instance, when working with medical data that is stored in healthcare data systems data perturbation approaches can be used to allow analysis that does not compromise the privacy of patient data. According to Wylde et al. (2022), integrating blockchain and smart contracts with privacy-preserving methods have strong adherence to cybersecurity and data privacy challenges which should respect legal frameworks like GDPR or ISO 27001.

Differential privacy has been successfully used in many domains one of which is healthcare since patients' data is often private. This paper shows how noise injection techniques help analyze patient demographics, disease occurrence and distribution, and treatment effectiveness without compromising patient privacy. A specific example of ED discussion applies to EHR systems with the help of differential privacy.

Combined with the addition of calibrated noise to queries on EHRs, hospitals and research institutions can collectively provide policy makers as well as other relevant stakeholders with aggregate analysis on the patient population without compromising on the individuated details of the patients.

According to Husnoo et al. (2021), differential privacy has been used to ensure IoT based healthcare systems, particularly privacy preserving approaches as an important means of protecting data from adversarial attacks. Such an approach minimises privacy threats while enabling enhancement of medical research and the delivery of out-patient services.

Table 3 Comparison of techniques

Mechanism/Scenario	**Laplace Noise**	**Gaussian Noise**	**Randomized Response**	**Privacy Budget Control**	**Blockchain Integration**
Numerical Queries	✓	✓	X	✓	✓
Categorical Data	X	X	✓	✓	X

High-Sensitivity Queries	X	✓	X	✓	✓
Real-Time Systems	X	X	✓	✓	✓
IoT-Enabled	✓	✓	X	✓	✓
GDPR/ISO 27001	✓	✓	✓	✓	✓
Healthcare Data	✓	✓	X	✓	✓
Survey Data	X	X	✓	✓	X
Statistical Aggregation	✓	✓	X	✓	✓
Attack Mitigation	✓	✓	X	✓	✓

Dalal and Roy (2021) explore the relationship of cybersecurity and privacy and point to the fact that amid today's issues, both these aspects should be balanced. They claim that the process of achieving this balance is rather difficult concerning the contemporary tendencies of the digital age, which put a great emphasis on privacy invasions.

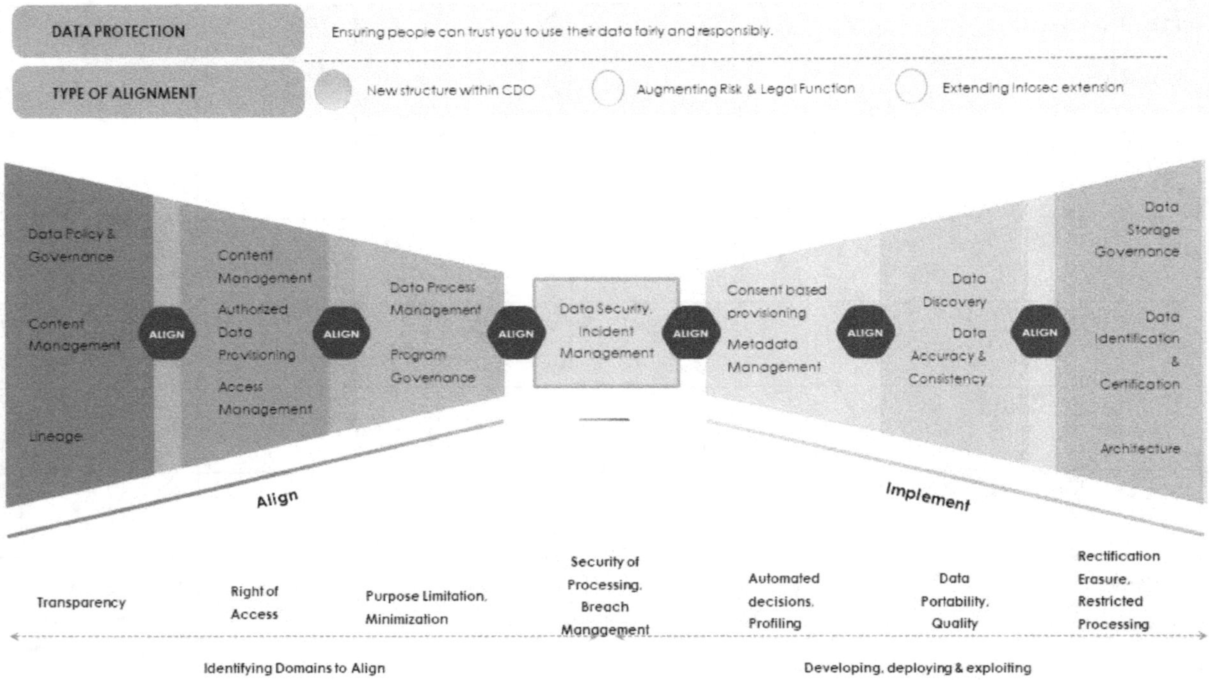

Figure 13 Data privacy and protection (Finextra Research, 2020)

This approach has plausibly solved this problem by affording strong privacy assurances and enabling data use by organizations. This capability is of significant value for the creation of the secure and sufficiently ethical systems considering the need for the privacy of individuals and the need for the corresponding needs for the modern applications based on the data.

This type of differential privacy can be advanced by enabling it with other technologies such as blockchain as shown in the table to enhance accountability and increase stakeholder's trust. In tackling these complex issues, differential privacy remains to be a critical force behind the future of data protection system.

3.3 Differential Privacy in AI

Adding DP to AI and machine learning has become crucial in controlling the privacy of data while preserving the utility of different models. Learning models with better privacy guarantees can be trained using differential privacy mechanisms including the differentially private stochastic gradient descent (DP-SGD).

For example, Ziller et al. (2021) have shown how the DP-SGD can be used for designing deep neural networks with compliance with privacy laws for medical imaging tasks. It can be said that their work focuses on the real-world applicability of DP implementations of open-source frameworks, including DP for per-sample gradients processing taking into account privacy constraints.

The use of DP in this respect aims at showing how privacy and utility may be achieved with minimum compromise, especially in such sectors like the health sector where issues of privacy have legal ramifications. However, the privacy loss accuracy trade-off remains a major difficulty in the application of DP to AI models.

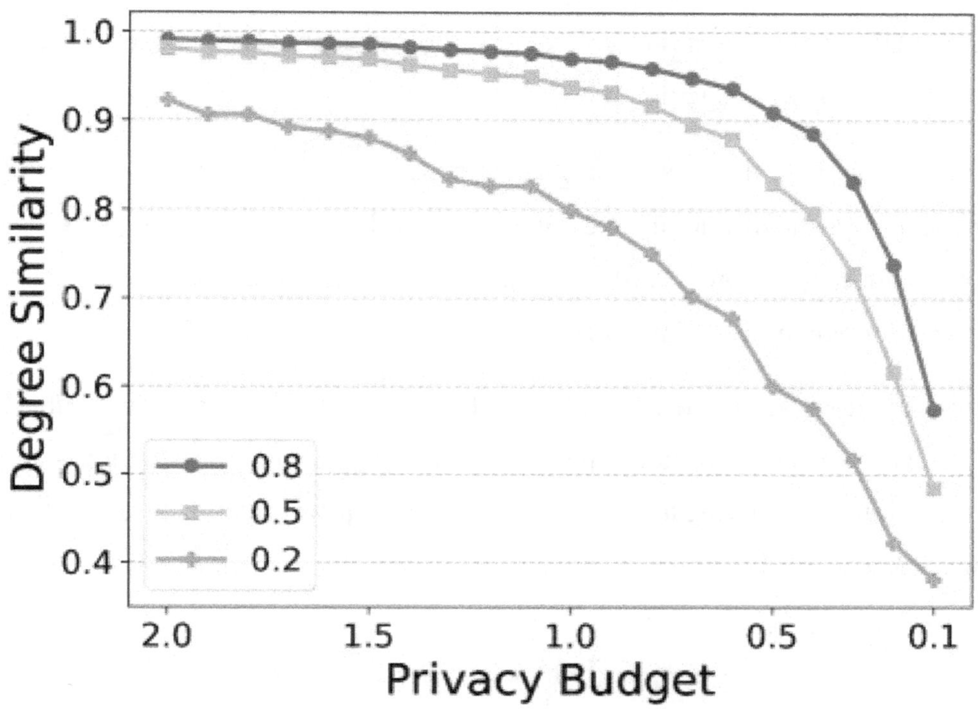

Figure 14 Differential Privacy Graph (arXiv, 2024)

Accordingly, Zhao et al. (2019) found membership inference and model extraction to be among the existing privacy attacks that require DP to be implemented across the layers of DL models. There we have the input layer, which is followed by the hidden layer and the output layer, into which DP mechanisms can be introduced. A strength of DP is that it offers mathematical correctness guarantees, although its benefits are not uniform across the model depending on the location of application.

Wu et al. (2020) also specified the relationship between accuracy and privacy by observing that out of sample differential privacy is inversely proportional to the square of the privacy budget and size of the training dataset. These results stress the necessity to properly set up privacy constraints for capturing the privacy levels of data and for sustaining model utility when many data owners contribute the model.

To attempt scalability and improve the DP integration, the concept of federated learning as a distributed training technique has been proposed. The intention in federating learning is that while data stays decentralized, the updates performed on the model also amalgamate at the center, in this method, privacy complications are contained.

In a related analysis, Boutin (2023) described NIST AI guidelines for differential privacy and information on trade-off involving privacy and utility. As such, this guidance will be useful for organisations that use privacy-preserving technologies (PETS) for big data processing. Thus, implementing DP provides an ability to make publicly available knowledge extracted from the sensitive data without violating privacy.

However, as it has been demonstrated in practice, specific implementations of differentially private models of artificial intelligence were successfully applied to various tasks in the real world. For instance, Johnston (2020) explained that businesses employ DP to help train AI in marketing while maintaining compliance with restrictive laws such as CCPA.

Such implementations are evidence for illustration of practicality of DP in dealing with two issues of privacy concern and model performance. They include making noise on gradients, avoiding identity transfer during training, and minimizing data revelation by adoption of privacy preserving methods.

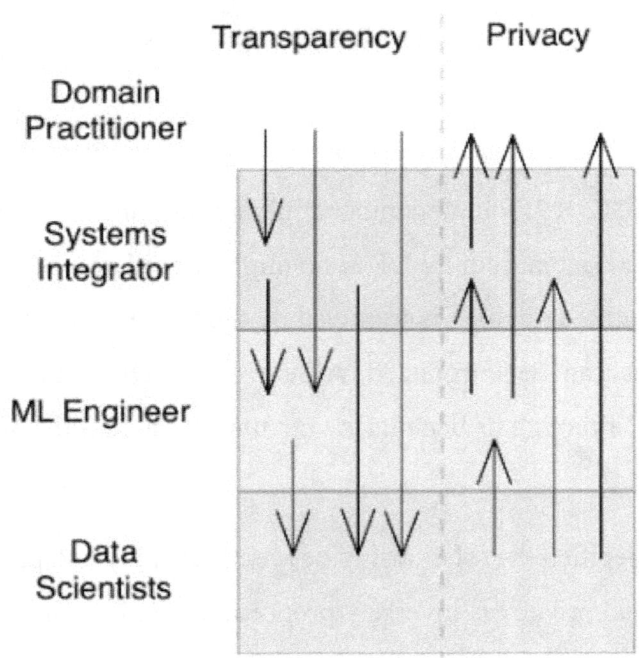

Figure 15 DP SDG Training (ResearchGate, 2021)

Some of the Significant advantages of DP in AI and ML.

- Defends the privacy of susceptible information of a user from being attacked.
- Protects the company from fines that may be occasioned by breach of data protection laws such as GDPR and HIPAA.
- Helps to provide partnership between organizations which have divorced datasets.
- Minimizes bias of data inputs into an ML algorithm since the input contains only anonymized data.

It is quite safe to say that the future of differential privacy in machine learning and AI and responsible data management Is to enhance scalability and create more elaborate and clear standard libraries. As advancement of AI applications remain constant, DP mechanism has a key role to portray in maintaining legal and technological compliance while addressing ethical challenges in implementing AI models for processing of sensitive data in various industries.

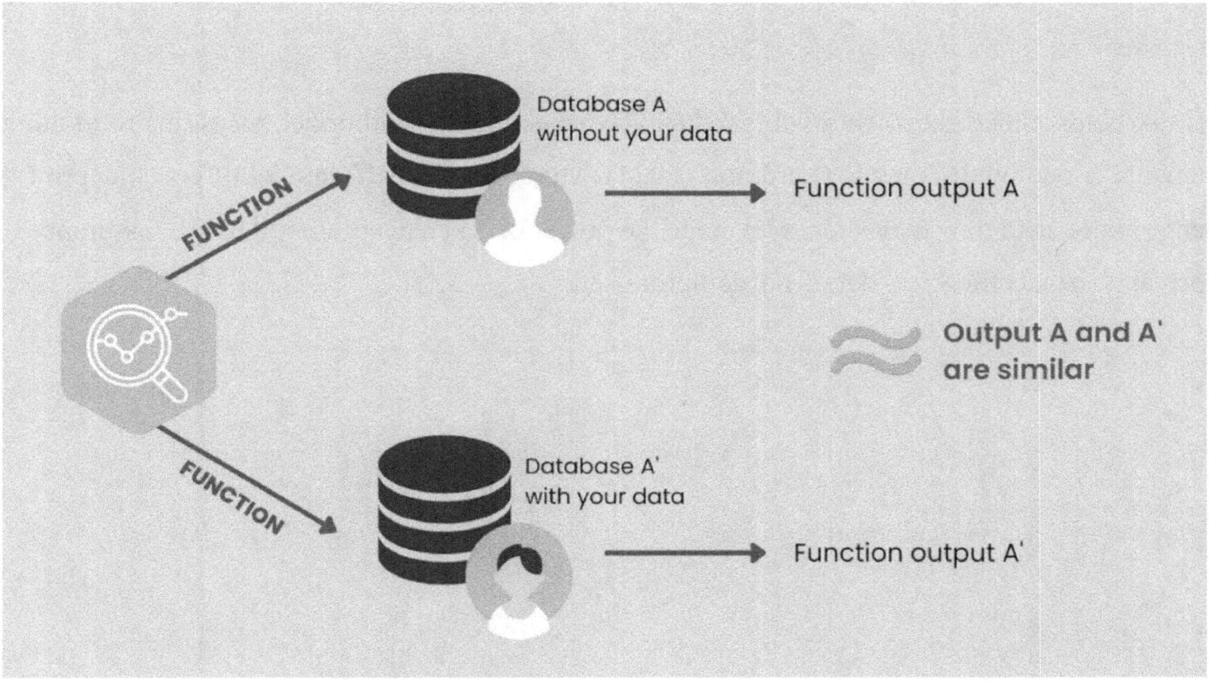

Figure 16 Differential Privacy in Machine Learning (Dr. Ernesto Lee, 2024)

3.4 Applications

There is no better method than DP that can help effectively protect user data stored on the cloud against the risks of data breaches. Since cloud-based systems still accumulate immense data belonging to organizations, privacy protection becomes essential. DP affirms the data can remain users' data, and organizations can run significant analyses.

At the forefront of this approach, there is the application of statistical noise and the control of a loss of privacy budget through which individual data contributions are hidden, but the overall dataset remains valuable (Bird, 2020).

Current cloud providers like Microsoft have been early adopters of DP within their solutions and services such as SmartNoise: It is an open-source framework introduced specifically to help the researchers and data scientists analyze and identify the patterns in the datasets and fulfill privacy-preserving obligations simultaneously.

Among the issues related to the usage of DP in order to protect data in the cloud, one of the main ones is the dilemma as to preserve the usefulness of the data while minimizing the information leakage. While cloud analytics is based on the premise of accessing large volumes of data to create value and insights, getting around compliance constraints often results in one: constraints. But SmartNoise and frameworks from organizations, such as PVML, have mitigations using retrieval-augmented generation (RAG), which examines data and does not transfer it.

It also helps to increase privacy while reducing worries about unauthorized access in the multiple tenants' cloud environments (Lardinois, 2024). Moreover, PVML's model offers blueprint to enterprises as to how they should leverage the power of AI analysis as well as the assurance of privacy, so that efficacy of data is not compromised.

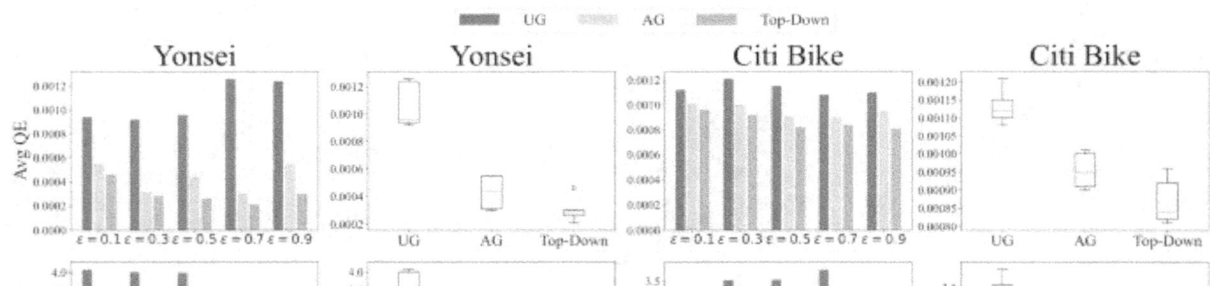

Figure 17 Real time privacy protection (Journal of Cloud Computing - SpringerOpen, 2022)

In collaborative cloud environments, DP assists secure sharing of data and can allow more than one organization to contribute data into cloud revolves for mutual and joint projects without infringing the privacy of each party. For example, in the ad tech and digital marketing sectors where third-party cookies are being de-scaled, DP becomes the foundation for privacy-centric ad models.

A good example of it is Google's Privacy Sandbox which is based on DP that provides targeted ads to large groups of users without leaking their particulars. This approach has a dual benefit of addressing the issue of consumer privacy while at the same time, fulfilling the essence of the market, that of competition and relevant advertisement placements (Schiff, 2020).

Major roles of DP in cloud-based security systems are as follows.

- Secure data sharing between organizations in the execution of joint activities.
- Privacy for inference attacks and data leakage during cloud analytics.
- Reduction of the level of compliance with data protection standards such as GDPR by anonymizing users' information.
- Avoiding the bias in machine learning by 'regulating' floor votes so that sensitive attributes don't sway the decision.

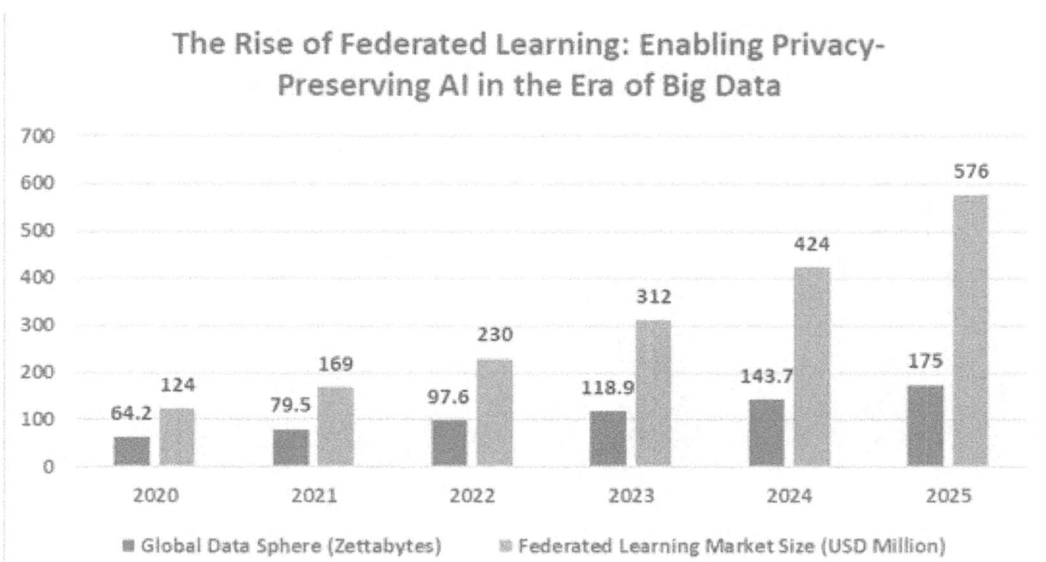

Figure 18 Rise of federated learning in privacy (IJRASET, 2024)

One example that clearly showed the capabilities of DP in cloud security is when applied for distributed AI and ML. According to Zhu et al. (2020), DP mechanisms improve security, provide stability to the training processes and provide equal distribution to the ML models. The use of DP in distributed ML systems gives organisations a practical and efficient method of data fusion while preserving protection in the analysis of data.

For instance, DP enables DP to control leaking of private information in collaborative AI, where multiple stakeholders contribute data. DP integration with cloud platforms is a revolutionary advance in privacy and security approaches.

DP does not only solve the privacy issue but also helps organizations maximize the benefits of their data by integrated innovation such as SmartNoise and distributed AI. By applying rigorous mathematical foundations in conjunction with DP concrete methodologies, DP provides a way for cloud privacy-sensitive applications that are feasible and do not entail sacrificing probabilistic modelling capability.

CHAPTER 4

Federated Learning

4.1 Overview

FL is a revolution to distributed machine learning, which allows a model training procedure on devices owned by multiple parties where the data never leaves the devices. In contrast to conventional AI-based systems, FL is designed to train models on devices while guaranteeing that the data is never centrally collected.

Shanmugam et al. (2023) have also described this decentralized structure as being based around such items of concern as model aggregation and communication overhead. For instance, FL used a central server to synchronize updates from other devices; hence it does not need to obtain raw data to learn the outcomes.

This approach is specifically beneficial when devising the capability of devices are different and the distribution of data is different and uncontrolled like IoT networks and healthcare systems. This enhances the levity of FL into the IoT networks, as demonstrated by Nguyen et al. (2021), to transform various applications.

IoT devices by nature are distributed thus an effective method in handling the inputs locally as seen in FL comes in handy for establishing protective services including attack detection, localization, and mobile crowdsensing without compromising the privacy of users. In the same way, Rahman et al. (2023) explain that in the health care context, FL with the incorporation of AI, and XAI can overcome adversarial threats on highly centralized structures of health care delivery.

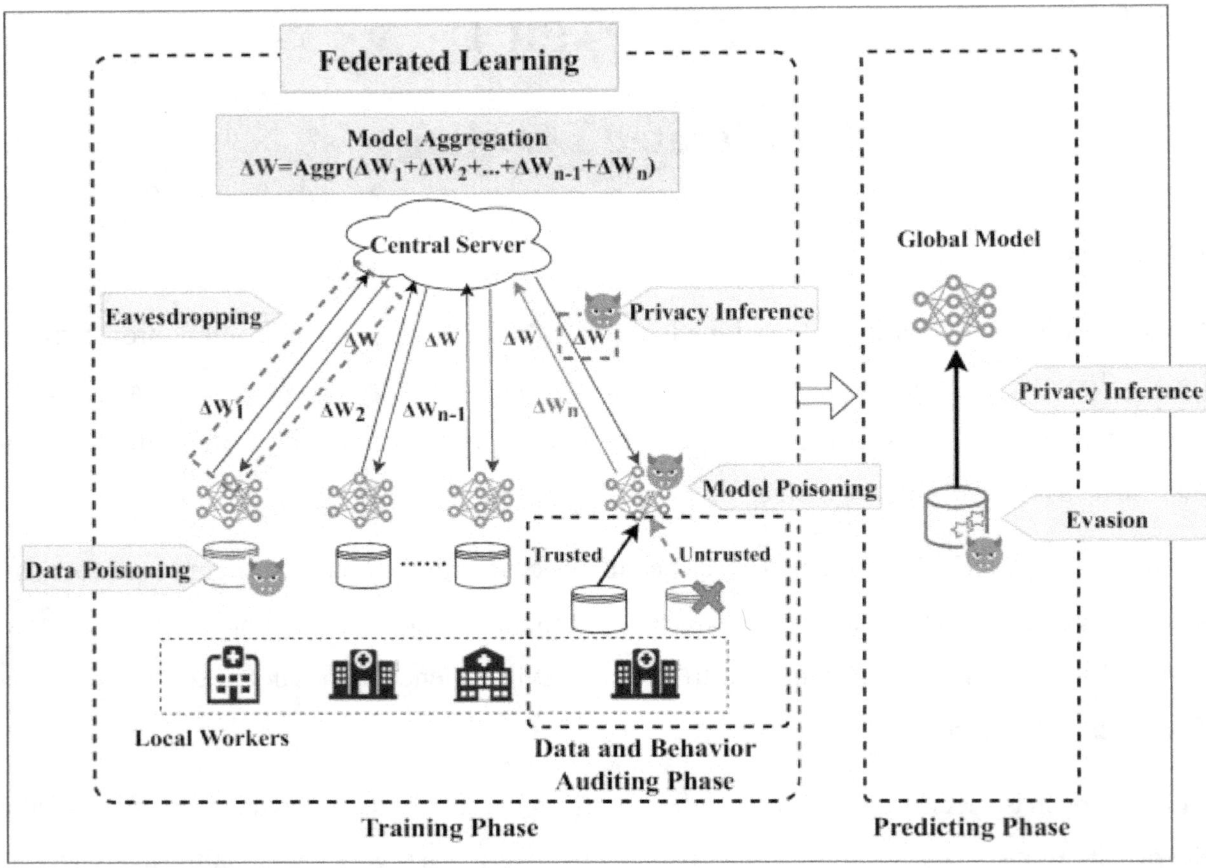

Figure 19 Federated Learning Model (Cybersecurity - SpringerOpen, 2022)

Using FL, strong communication is enabled between the devices and raw patient data does not have to be transmitted, all of which improves the privacy and reliability in use in medical applications. For instance, FL is being applied to train disease diagnosis and recommendations models for treatments, promote data sharing across hospitals, and reduce the data leak risks at the same time.

The comparative analysis of FL's applications based on the domains of its usage can be described in the following manner.

Table 4 Federated Learning applications

Domain	Applications	Key Benefits
IoT Networks	Data sharing mechanisms, attack detection, smart cities, and UAV's	Improved capacity along with privacy and security
Healthcare	Disease cold case, targeted treatment, and team diagnosis	Greater security, stability and less vulnerability of data.

Consumer Devices	On-screen profiles, next-word prediction, voice recognition and on-device machine learning (e.g. primary Google Assistant).	It identified localized learning and limited data exposure as factors impacting organizations.
Neural Architecture Search	Optimising the hierarchy of federated neural architecture	Automatic selection of values of model parameters

As Zhu et al. (2021) proposes, federated neural architecture search aims at optimizing deep neural networks within frameworks of FL. This technique effectively eliminates the need for tuning hyperparameters and model architectures, and it guarantees that FL can obtain high accuracy regardless of efficient computation from a centralized source.

A particularly meaningful application of federated neural architecture search is in conditions where data heterogeneity is paramount such as smart cities or industrial IoT. Another such example is Google using FL for improving on-device Machine Learning, which Dilmegani (2024) has explained. This way, FL keeps personal data safe to train models such as "Hey Google" on user devices directly thus preserving user privacy.

It has been shown in this application how FL would help improve the user interface with the highest privacy standards intact making it a pillar for future AI systems. However some difficulties are still encountered in the large scale use of FL. According to Shanmugam et al. (2023), communication overhead, model aggregation, and security issues are the major challenges.

Solving such challenges needs improvements in efficient aggregation protocols, secure encryption approaches and anti-adversary attacks. Also, Rahman et al. (2023) notes that issues of consistency and dependability are essential for FL systems and more so in sensitive areas such as healthcare due to data impartiality and reliability.

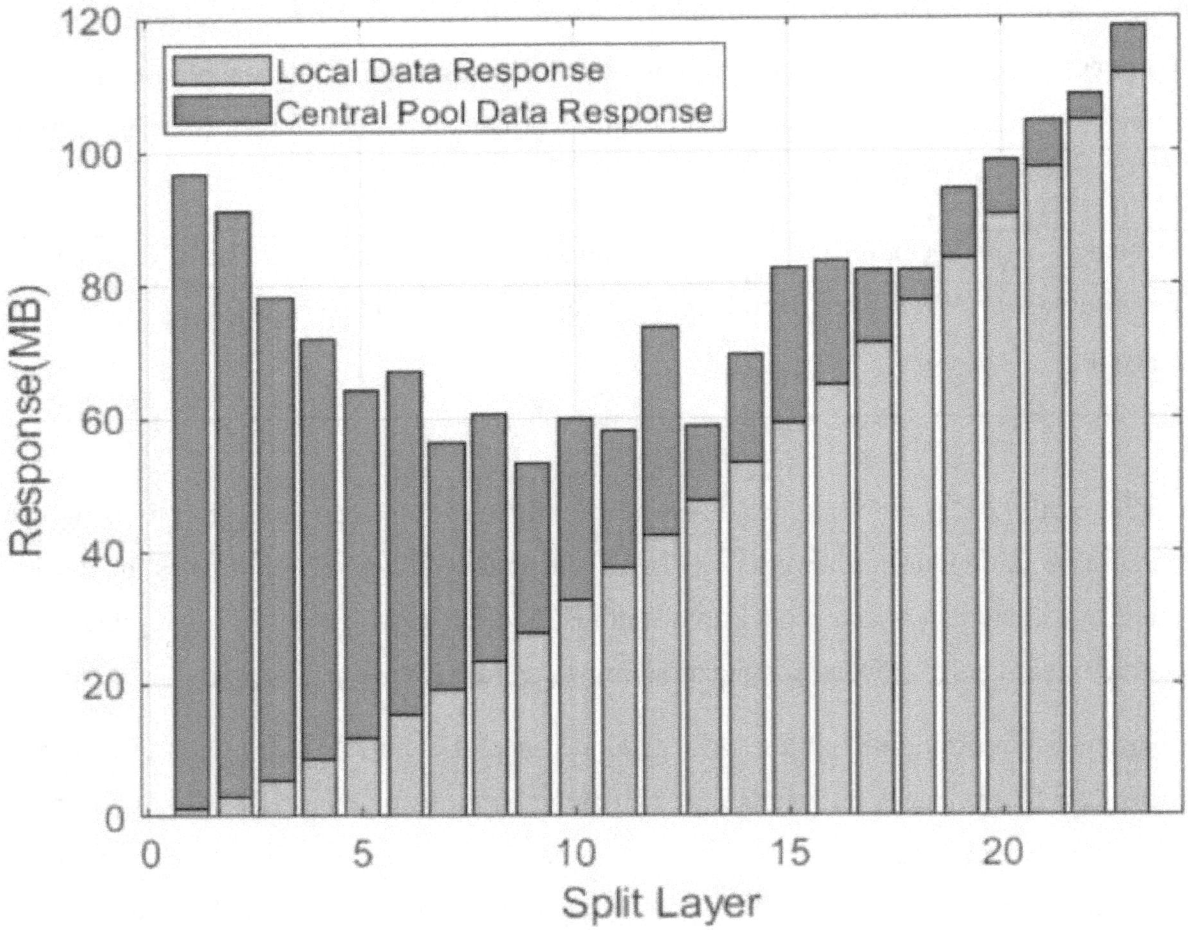

Figure 20 Federated Learning for network attack (Nature, 2024)

The FL's approach to learning delivers revolutionary features for privacy-enhanced artificial intelligent applications in different fields. In this way, FL as a means of collaborative intelligence without data leakage makes use of data in a totally different paradigm than before. Nonetheless, while the advantages of GPT-2 remain apparent, it is necessary to overcome the corresponding technical and operational problems to apply it widely in secure, more significant AI applications.

4.2 Benefits

FL has thus developed to be an effective weapon in cybersecurity while presenting various prospects for improving data privacy, avoiding data loss while transferring information securely especially in intense areas such as healthcare, finance, and cloud computing.

FL's greatest advantage can be secured in its distributed structures that help to keep the sensitive data stored locally on the individual devices while training on the amalgamated models take place. This feature alone reduces the dangers of concentrating data sets in one location, which is a topology preferred by hackers.

Due to the manner of data processing in FL where model updates are only shared instead of raw data, there is a high improvement of privacy and security among industries where data sensitivity plays a crucial role (Ferrag et al., 2021). For example, In healthcare, FL allows training of AI models in one hospital or research centre and another without having to exchange patient information, which may be a problem from the viewpoint of laws and ethics.

Adopting FL into cybersecurity likewise supports the safe identification and counteraction of threats in extensive networks. Centralized models have some problems such as time delay in responding to new threats and data centralization.

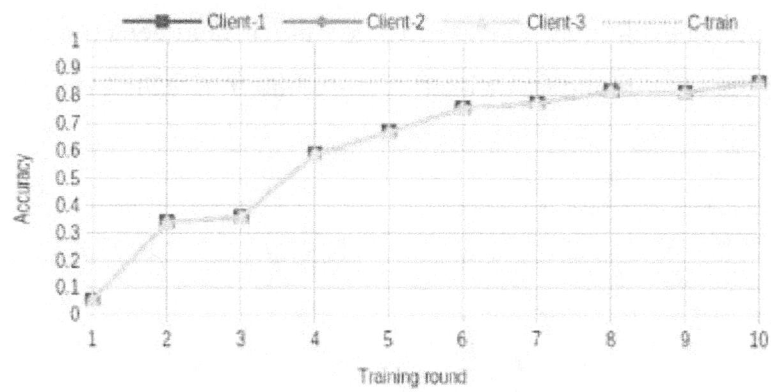

(a) Full-aggregation learning

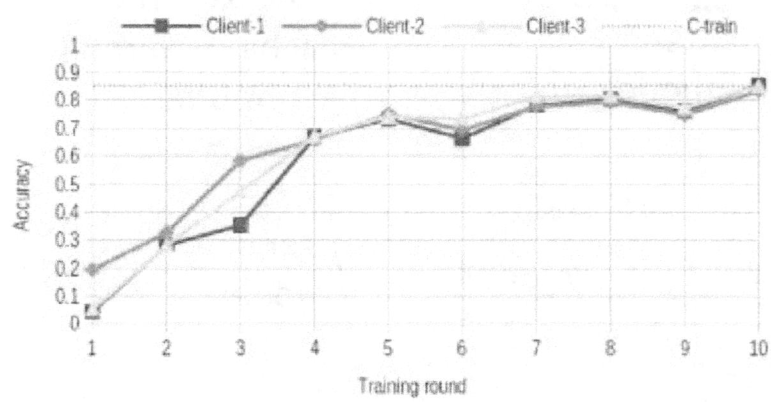

(b) Partly-aggregation learning

Figure 21 Federated Learning and malware identification (ACM Digital Library - Association for Computing Machinery, 2022)

FL, on the other hand, gives an opportunity to react immediately with identified threats because of utilizing the specific data processing elements located nearby. This becomes beneficial in the use cases such as IDS IoT-FL where FL improves the training accuracy of DL models together with maintaining data privacy (Ferrag et al., 2022).

Furthermore, FL has combined with various techniques such as differential privacy technique, homomorphic encryption technique, and block chain for enhancing security aspects of Firefox. All these methods ensure that not even the model updates that are exchanged throughout the training process are vulnerable to adversarial manipulation or leakage of data (Khurana & Kaul, 2019).

Another domain in which FL is bringing significant progress in cybersecurity is the financial technology (FinTech) industry. FL solves the problem of data privacy and allows safe data sharing and analysis without violating the provisions of legislation in the sphere of FinTech.

According to FL, this helps financial institutions to train a fraud detection model at one branch or institution with the other branches or institutions without revealing the transactions information.

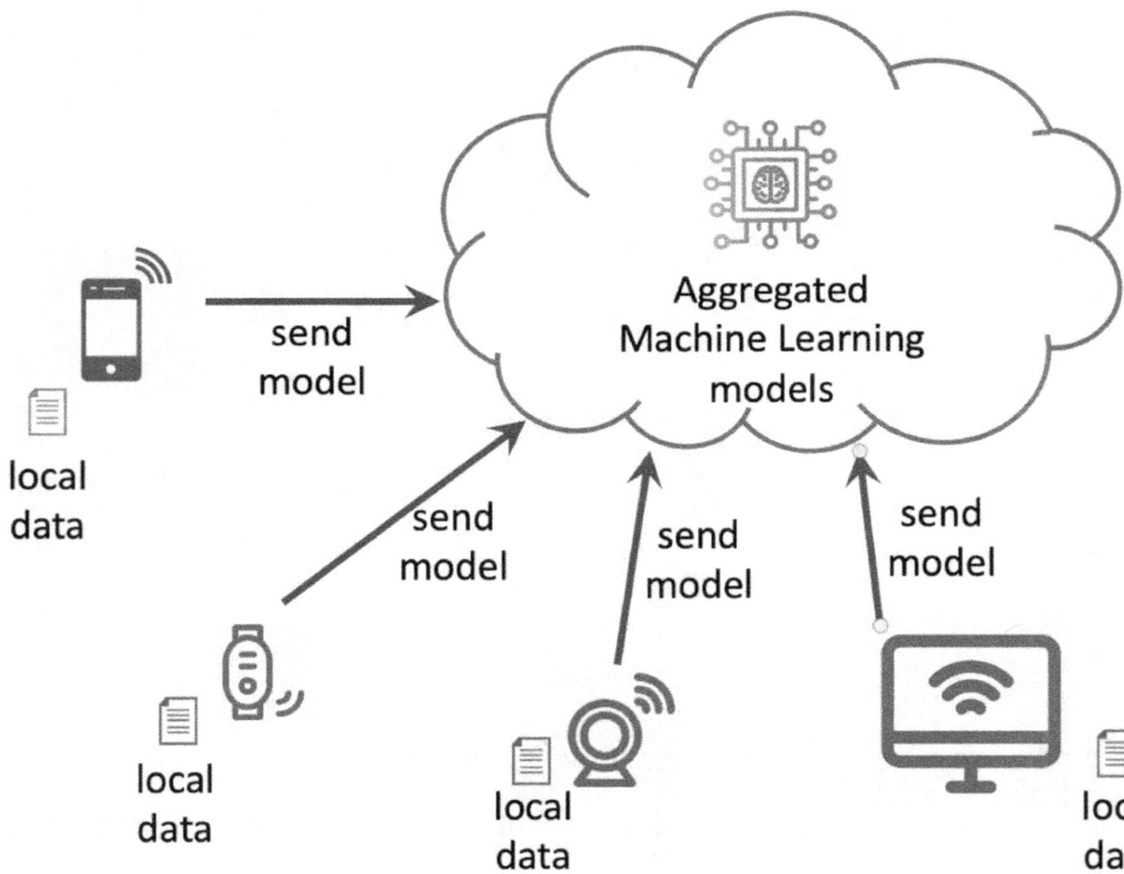

Figure 22 Federated Learning through blockchain (arXiv, 2024)

This not only decreases the likelihood of fraudulent data entry but also enhances the chances of efficient fraudulent detection through improved model training and subsequent risk analytics, as the datasets are combined and diverse, unlike what normally happens in traditional applications of machine learning where datasets are often segmented and thus small (Dash et al., 2022). Moreover, the openness characteristic of FL through the use of XAI makes it possible for the user and organizations to trust in the models without compromising on the security aspect of the innovation.

- Data privacy: Decentralized processing calms down the risks of data leakage due to the absence of centralized data storage centers.
- Reduced breach risks: FL vanishes the attack surface probability by allowing the exchange of only the aggregate of the model updates.
- Threat detection: FL-based systems can detect an attack in real-time and lever from FL decentralized and distributed model training.
- Data-sharing: FL makes secure collaborations possible in highly sensitive industries such as health and financial services and yet is fully compliant with the rules on the protection of privacy.
- Advanced security: Combination with homomorphic encryption, differential privacy, and blockchain strengthens the model and defends against adversarial attacks.

Some of the roles of FL in cybersecurity can best be explained by considering IoT and Industrial IoT (IIoT). since IoT devices are computing nodes they produce huge amounts of data, thus centralized systems pose issues of scalability, latency and privacy.

To these challenges FL proposes to resolve them through training on edge devices in a distributed manner so as to cut down on data traffic and increase system throughput. For instance, the Edge-IIoTset dataset shows how FL is capable of performance improvement compared to usual centralized systems in the case of cybersecurity, such as DoS attacks, malware, and injection attacks. This work had sought to introduce a new model for protecting IoT networks through building FL-based models trained on this dataset, which would elevate the accuracy level without compromising data privacy (Ferrag et al., 2022).

Therefore, FL becomes central to modern cybersecurity applications as it opens ways to secure the data-sharing, furthering privacy, and empowering collaborative AI training. The adoption of this practice across sectors further shows its potential of reshaping not only cybersecurity but also preventing privacy loss and the impact on solutions' performance and to GDPR legislation.

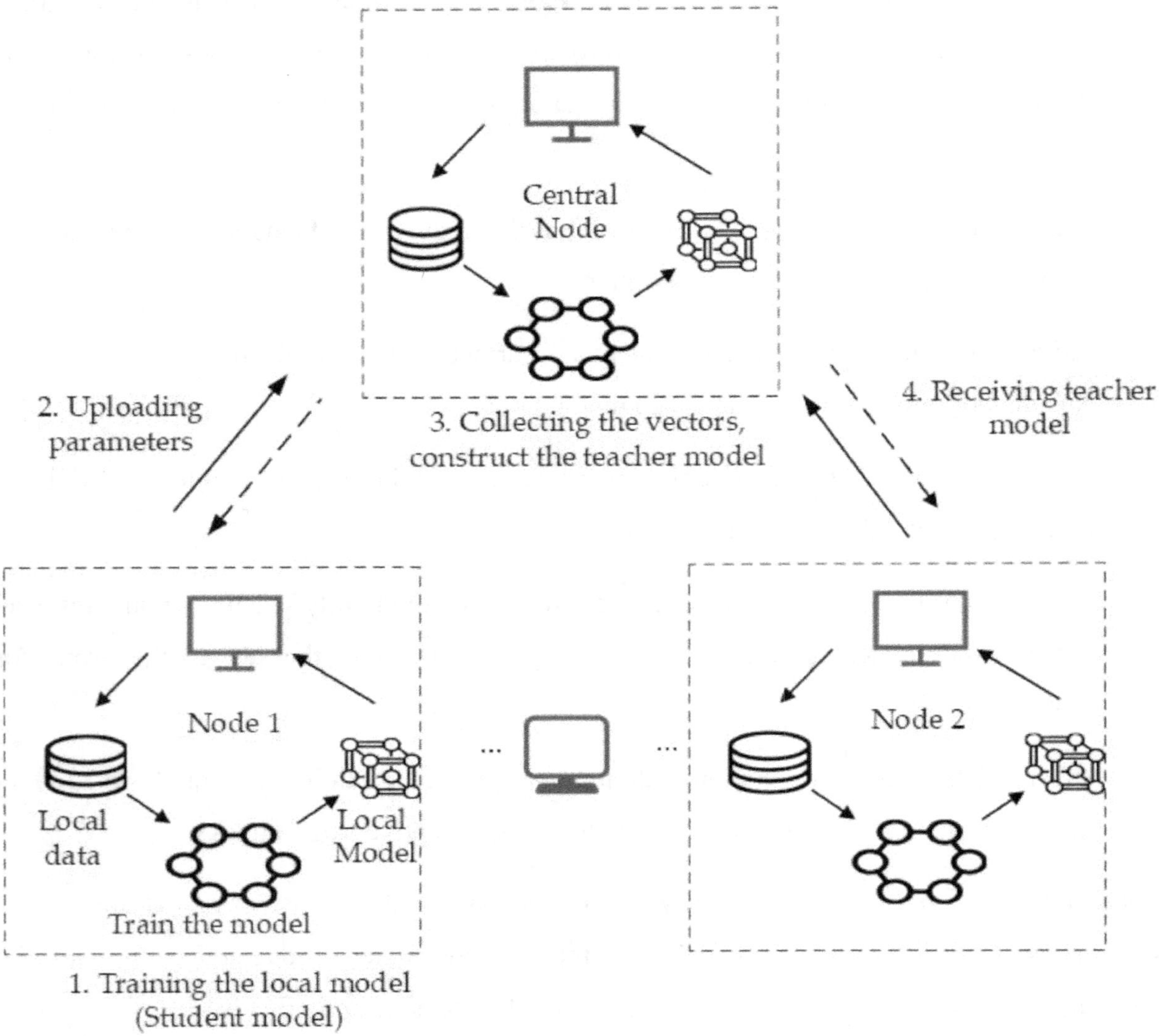

Figure 23 Decentralised Federated Learning (MDPI, 2023)

4.3 Challenges

The main advantage of using Federated Learning (FL) in cloud-based cybersecurity includes; Nevertheless, it encounters several technical, operational, and regulatory issues essential to enhance the application of FL to its maximum capability. These include privacy, security and compliance issues within which functionality and efficiency are maximized whilst cost and time are minimized.

Another technical problem that deserves special mention in the framework of FL in cloudbased cybersecurity is communication overhead. In a FL setup, the model updates are exchanged between the central aggregator and, on the other hand, the participants, and this would incur a lot of bandwidth usage &talent; particularly in instances where multiple devices and participants are involved.

This becomes more severe whenever devices present in areas of limited resources like the IoT systems are affected. Yaacoub et al. (2023) explain that devices in IoT networks are diverse, and they may not be synchronized, leading to challenges in the execution of FL models.

The communication overhead does not only reduce model performances but also increases the time needed for threat detection which is very prohibitive when using real time applications. Such challenges need to be addressed through the use of better algorithms and techniques of data compression so as to relieve the burden on the communication net.

The other significant problem is the model fidelity across different and varying devices. In cloud-based environments data are split over a heterogeneous set of devices that may have different computational and data characteristics. Such diversity can lead to Model Convergence issues or where the global model may be poor since one participant contributes significantly more data than the other.

Zhang et al. (2022) pointed out that adversarial attacks and malicious participants will make this problem more severe and influence the reliability and credibility of the federated model. A significant challenge therefore is to get data of consistent quality across the devices in order to arrive at the final model that is accurate and able to flag threats as and when they emerge.

To tackle this challenge, new sophisticated aggregation methods should be created and differential privacy or SMC introduced to guarantee data quality and model performance.

FL applied to cloud-based cybersecurity also comes with operational issues about security threats. While FL assists in sustaining privacy because information is held in localized, FL is vulnerable to attacks. The adversarial threats leading to FL model poisoning include Deep Gradient Leakage, and GAN-based attacks.

Zhang et al. (2022) point out that the local model can be malafied by these attacks to cause model poisoning and leak sensitive data. One of the main threats that arise from malicious participants or a dishonest aggregator is the potential for the entire federated learning mechanism to be attacked.

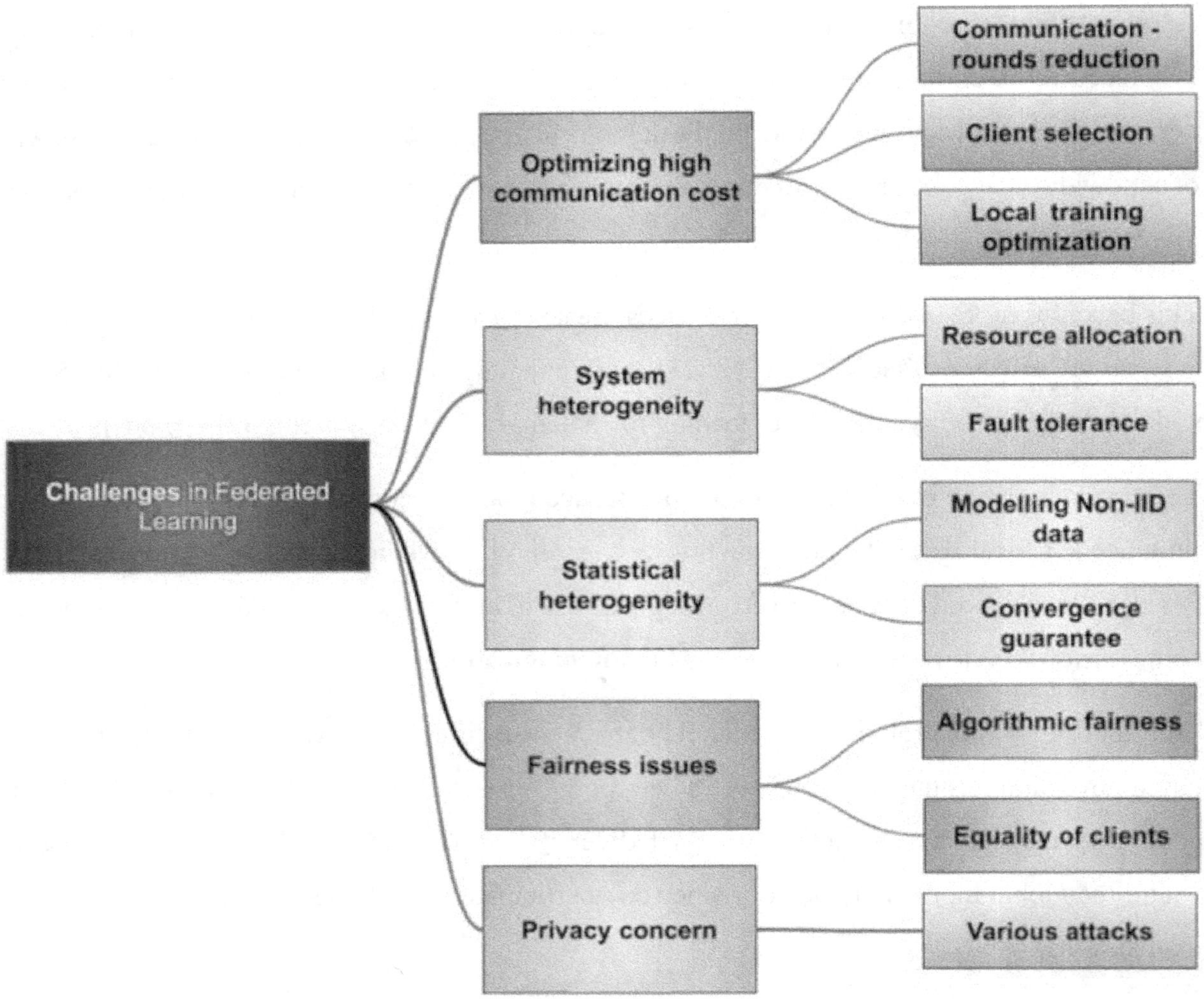

Figure 24 Challenges in Federated Learning (link.springer.com, 2024)

To reduce these risks, the implementation of other security features that can help to protect against adversarial threats, and guarantee the safeguarding of the federated model are considered, for instance, blockchain or Trusted Execution Environments (TEEs).

Overall, a number of regulatory issues intensify the implications of FL for cloud-based cybersecurity operations. Due to the fact that FL operates on a global level, it is rather challenging to fulfill legislations of data protection such as GDPR in Europe and CCPA in California.

FL must also make sure data privacy is kept while also making sure that it complies with legal requisites of each jurisdiction. As an example, in the Healthcare sector with reference to Nvidia's Clara solution, Dilmegani, (2024) pointed out that, through FL, training can be conducted without the actual data being shared. Alternative, organizations have to consider a legal issue of data siting, cross border data transfer, and localization, which may significantly differ from country to country.

Table 5 Challenges in Federated Learning

Challenge	**Communication Overhead**	**Model Accuracy**	**Security Vulnerabilities**	**Regulatory Compliance**	**Heterogeneity of Devices**	**Data Privacy**
Communication Overhead						
Model Accuracy						
Security Vulnerabilities						
Regulatory Compliance						
Heterogeneity of Devices						
Data Privacy						
Cross-border Data Transfers						
Integration with Existing Systems						
Real-time Data Processing						

Model Training Efficiency						

Federated Learning holds tremendous potential in cloud-based cybersecurity; however, to realise this potential, the approach has several challenges that require close consideration. Addressing issues like communication overhead, model accuracy, security threats and other regulatory issues is only possible if researchers, practitioners and the regulatory agencies come together to find better, safer and legal way of doing things.

4.4 Cloud Security

Federated Learning (FL) is a breakthrough innovation in machine learning especially in the aspect of strengthening the cloud security and privacy. Its structure enables for the efficient use of its capacities in organizations, where the data has to be protected from others, for example, in the sphere of medicine or finance.

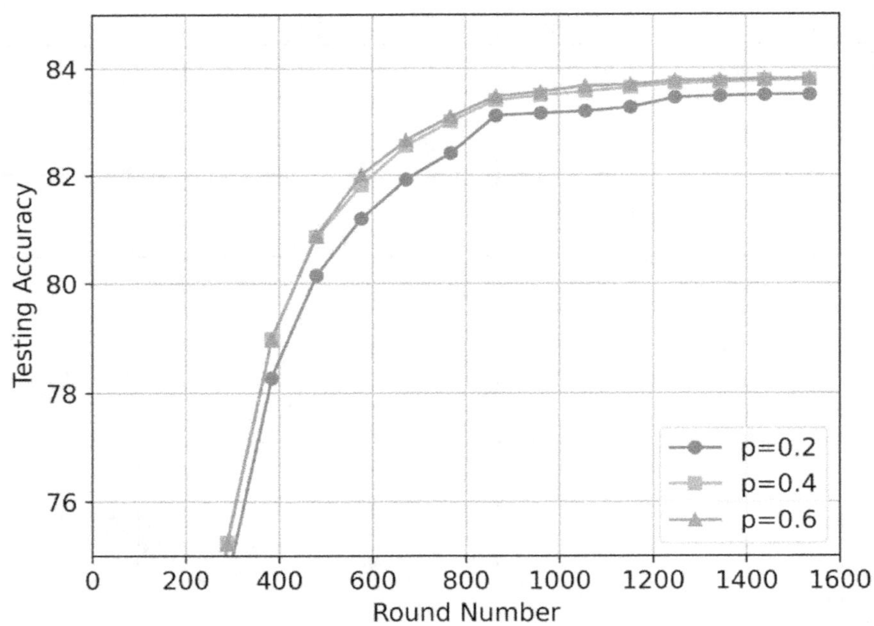

Figure 25 Low latency federated learning (IEEE Computer Society, 2024)

FL provides coordination capability for the construction of models collaboratively based on training data but does not need the actual data to be transferred between different devices and thus prevents users' privacy information from leakage (Wen et al., 2023). However, updates of models are transmitted instead, and this is a significant enhancement to the conventional centralized artificial neural network learning method. Especially as more cloud platforms process huge quantities of sensitive data, FL's ability to function as a module within existing platforms to offer privacy-guaranteeing AI solutions becomes more attractive

But nonetheless there are some technical and operational concerns to effectively applying FL in cloud environments. Network overhead is one of the main challenges as all units have to continuously report to the main server based on changes noticed by the units.

This can be stressing the network resources especially at the time of handling large data in a constrained environment. However, since there is the involvement of a large number of diverse devices including IoT networks which are highly diverse, training may become difficult.

Due to the variability in computation capacities across the devices, the performance of the model may differ (Bao et al., 2022). These disparities warrant algorithms that would address the diverse device strength among the participating clientele. The above factors can pose a threat to FL under conditions of cybersecurity in cloud-based applications in terms of efficiency and scalability.

Beside with the performance, the issue of security are also other concerns that need to be discuss in relation to FL. Despite a bonus of improved privacy compared to traditional models of web apps, FL remains vulnerable to specific kinds of attacks. For instance, adversarial attackers can attempt to manipulate the updates from the participants to insert a bias or else an intention error in the global model.

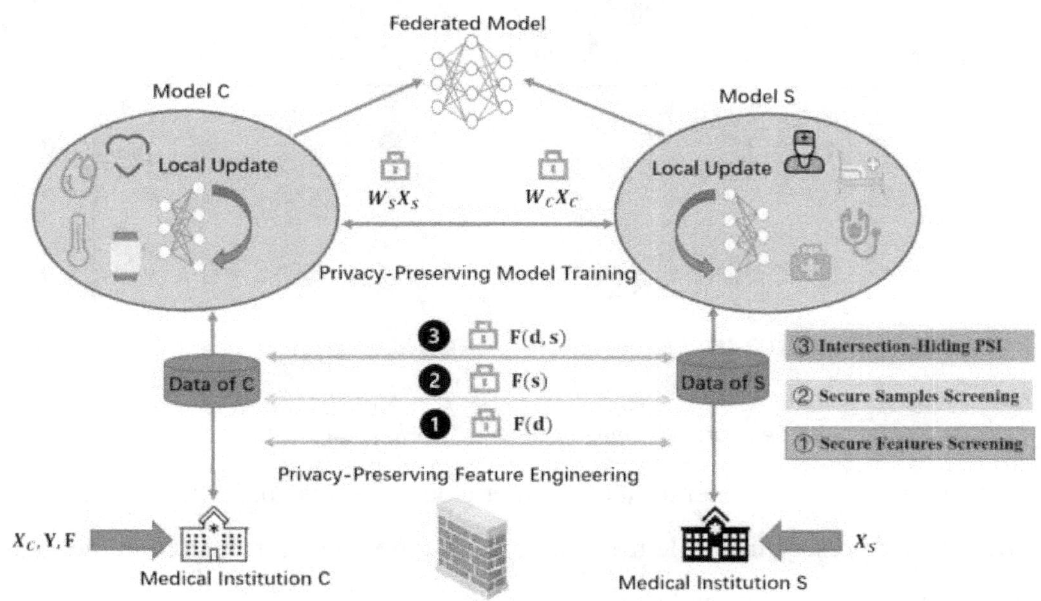

Figure 26 Vertical federated learning (Cybersecurity - SpringerOpen, 2023)

Two specific types pose a high threat: Deep Gradient Leakage, and GAN attacks as they enable extraction of participants' sensitive information while, in most cases, the attackers do not require direct access to the raw data (Bouacida & Mohapatra, 2021, Zhang et al., 2021). These threats require that strong security that involves encryption or any differential privacy method to be implemented to ensure that the model being used is not compromised by the participants' information that is sent in the process of the update.

The mostly important issues associated with FL are security and privacy, therefore, are more important to address these concerns to use FL in the learning environment more often. The environment regulation also has a critical influence in the use of FL in cloud security deployment. When there is an increasing trend towards data protection, especially in jurisdictions such as the European Union where the GDPR law applies, such compliance becomes a complicated matter.

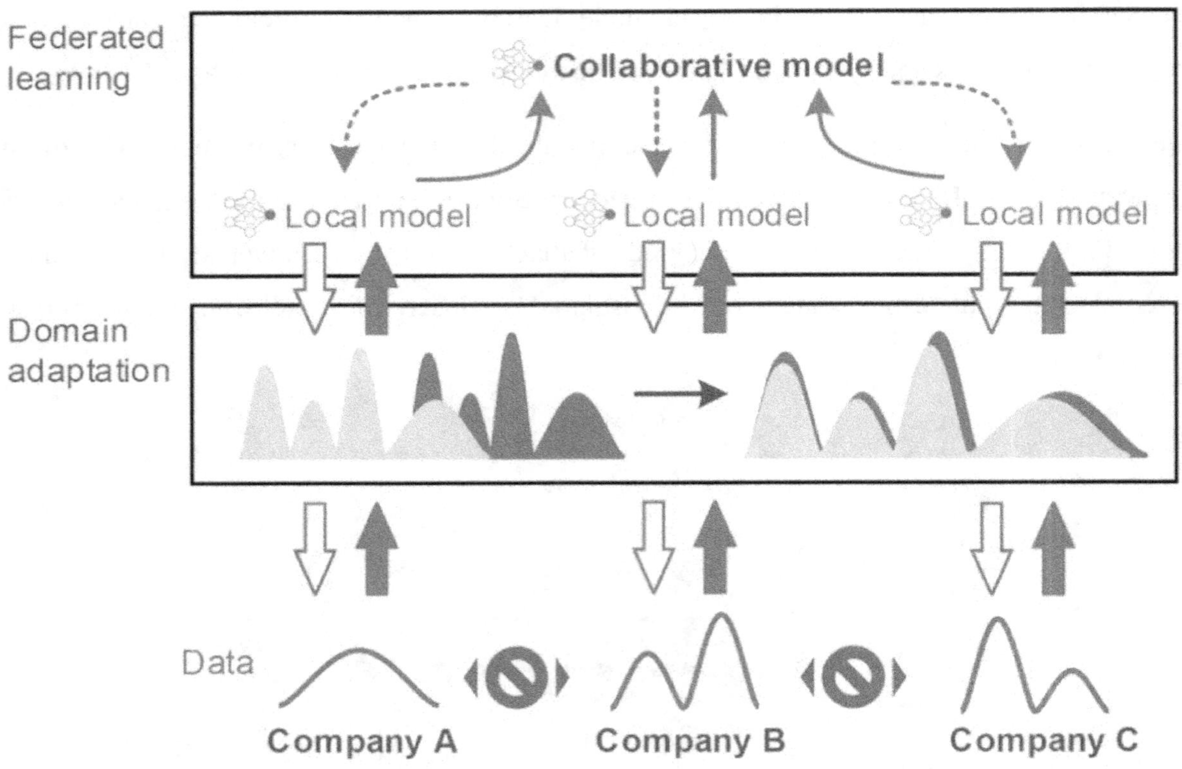

Figure 27 Federated learning in coporate world (ResearchGate, 2021)

Since FL training entails the generation of synthetic data that resembles real data, it must be made to be privacy-preserving while meeting legal requirements formulated in the regulation concerning the usages, storage, and sharing of data.

This entails frequent changes to synthesise and enhance FL systems to adhere to new privacy regulations (Mammen, 2021). When data sovereignty debates come clearly to the front, it will always be difficult to follow regional data protection laws while gaining the advantages provided by the federated learning models.

Researchers have proposed different ideas to address these problems to improve the security of FL systems. For instance, in order to deliver decentralized distribution of the model updates, the involvement of blockchain technology for the purpose of verification of the model altruism was recommended in (Zhang et al., 2022). Moreover, Trusted Execution Environments (TEEs) provide an isolated platform for FL algorithms with no peeking over the data in the training procedure.

Key Challenges:

- Efficiency overhead in the transmission and load on the network (Wen et al., 2023).
- Model performance is reduced by the heterogeneity of these devices (Bao & Guo, 2022).
- Threats, other risks and inclinations including adversarial attacks (Bouacida & Mohapatra, 2021).
- Privacy and protection of personal data (Mammen 2021).

Nevertheless, Federated Learning also includes several issues that should be addressed to serve cloud security and privacy-preserving AI. Realization on actual environments, therefore, will therefore requires answering the following questions to enable FL systems deliver appealing cybersecurity besides maintaining privacy and data functionality for training.

CHAPTER 5

Implementation

5.1 Overview

Homomorphic encryption, differential privacy, and FL are all expedient techniques to scale privacy-preserving AI in the cloud setting for cybersecurity applications. These technologies collectively play the role of data protection while enhancing the flow of AI model training. The federated learning permits the training process to happen locally and data remaining on the local devices which is a plus in healthcare and finance sectors since they involve sensitive data (Wen et al., 2023; Mammen, 2021).

Another layer of protection provided by homomorphic encryption is the ability it provides to work on data itself in an encrypted form to compute results directly from encrypted datasets rather than decrypting the data to perform the computation before encrypting it again. The use of these methods gives a strong system for providing privacy while still incorporating all of the necessary features.

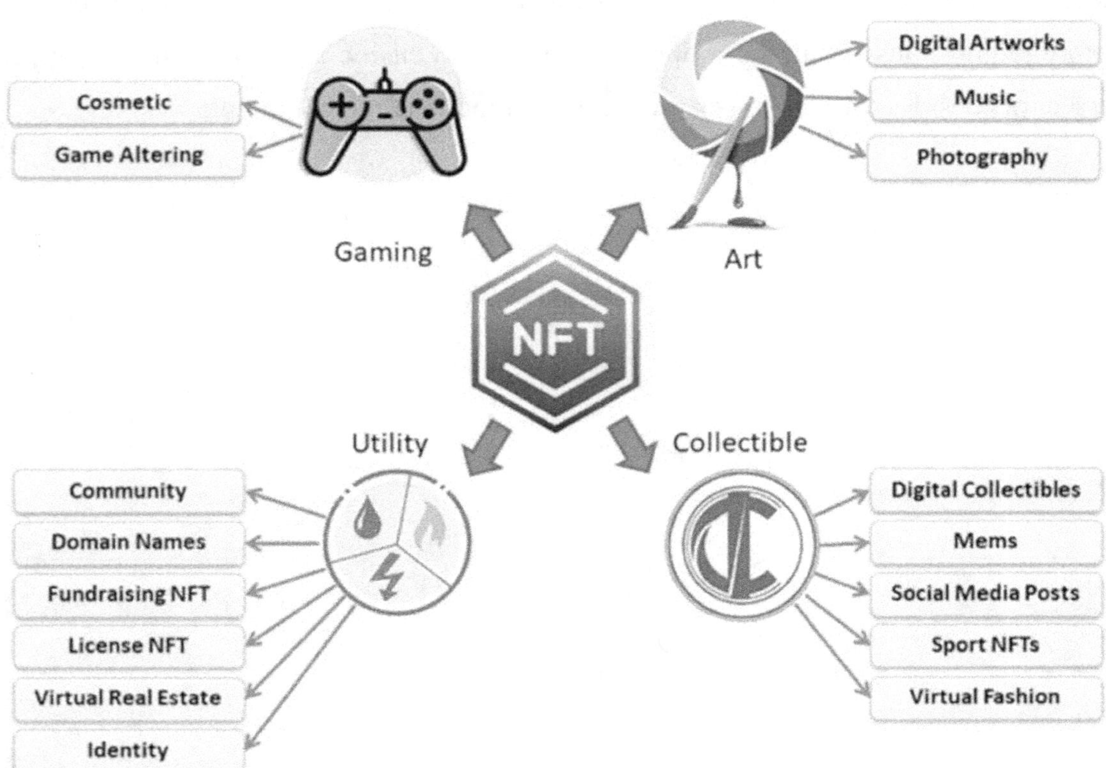

Figure 28 Cybersecurity in AI Metaverse (MDPI, 2022)

For instance, healthcare institutions that work on prognostic models for non-common diseases would have legal and ethical issues to share patient information. These institutions for instance are in a position to train AI models through federated learning without having data centralized (Bao & Guo, 2022). Homomorphic encryption preserves the operations on that data encrypted, so that even in training, nobody gives access to it.

Differential privacy serves this setup to anonymize data outputs, and thereby, prevent data subjects from being identified as illustrated by Wen et al. (2023). Same technique is applied in the finance where in fraud detection system transaction data is required to be undisclosed. When these technologies are integrated, institutions can train reliable models, given regulatory standards.

However, there are some challenges this integration as well. One drawback that has so far received much attention is the high cost of computation that arises from homomorphic encryption. As Yaacoub et al. (2023) notes, encrypted computations in resource limited environment such as IoT systems are a challenge.

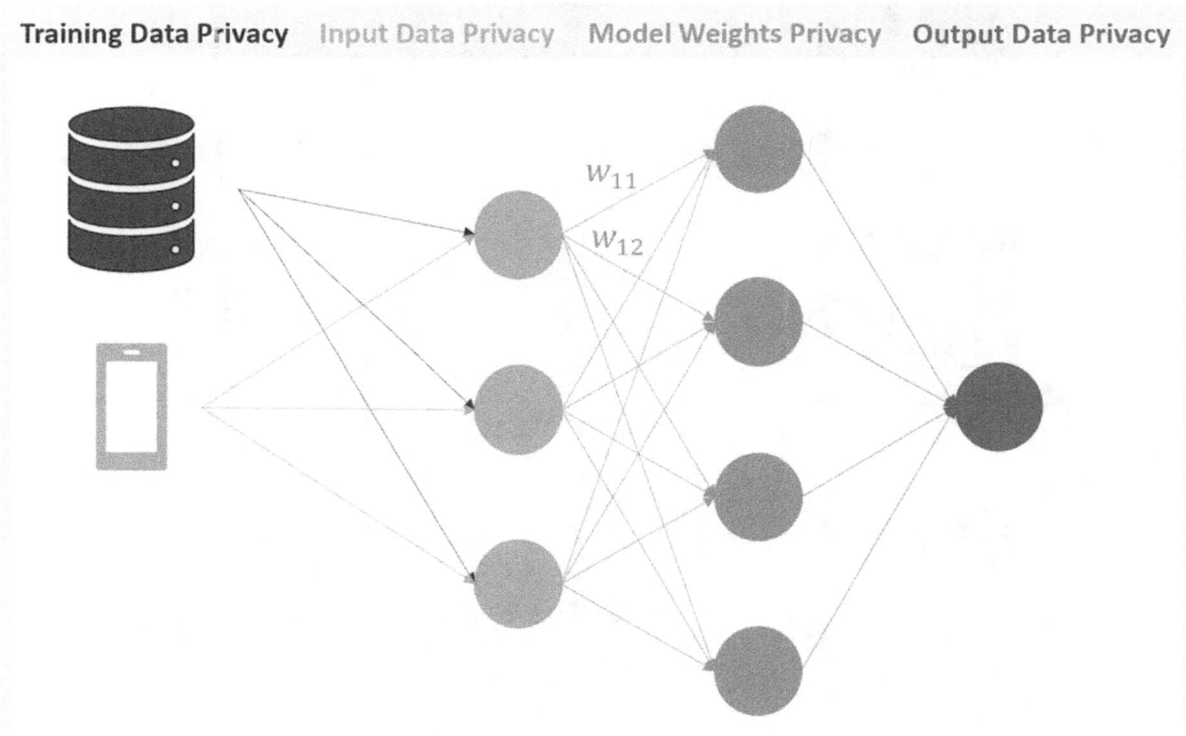

Figure 29 Privacy-Preserving Model (Towards Data Science, 2020)

In such settings, federated learning also faces heterogeneity of devices where some are powerful while others are weak in computational and connectivity. Furthermore, as Zhang et al. (2022) explain, FL systems are also susceptible to such advanced attacks as gradient leakage and adversarial exploits. All these threats require a strong pre-emptive measure that include the use of encryption and privacy preserving measures to curb them.

Examples of these challenges and how they may be addressed are presented by the following case studies. For example, Nvidia's Clara platform on how use federated learning with encryption to support model training across various healthcare systems (Dilmegani, 2024). As such, through adoption of homomorphic encryption, Clara guarantees that patient data confidentiality is maintained while promoting the creation of worldwide models.

Differential privacy also provides a degree of extra protection, in which patient data are anonymous even if intermediate model parameters are revealed to the adversary. Likewise, Bao & Guo (2022) tackle cloud-edge collaborative architecture and show that such technologies are feasible particularly in scenarios that cannot harness centralized processing because of latency or security issues.

Figure 30 AI-based cybersecurity (MDPI, 2023)

Such challenges are being tackled in future research through improved encryption techniques, and communication procedures. In particular, Bouacida and Mohapatra (2021) highlight the requirements for defense mechanisms that introduce significant sophisticated encryption protocols that have a lesser processing burden and yet are a competent defense in opposition to threats. Also, future frameworks combining blockchain with federated learning are being developed to improve the level of trust and openness in such decentralized processes even further (Zhang et al., 2022).

Cybersecurity on cloud holds a great potential of homomorphic encryption, differential privacy, and federated learning together. Through these technologies, it becomes possible for organisations to benefit from AI while at the same time protecting the privacy of consumers data and being in compliance with current and future legal requirements. Altogether this harmony opens the future for the development of safe and privacy-preserving applications of AI.

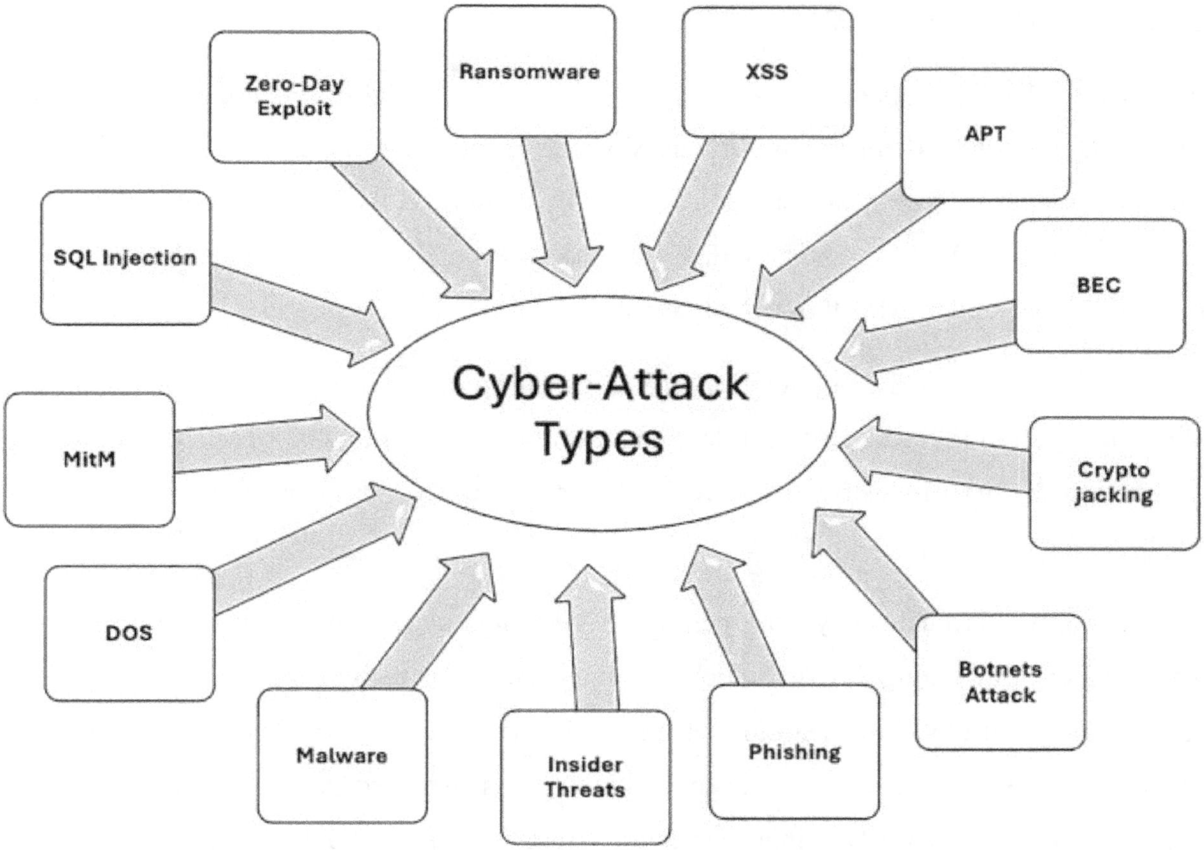

Figure 31 Cyber-attacks types (Journal of Big Data - SpringerOpen, 2024)

5.2 Frameworks and tools

The continuous growth of artificial intelligence (AI) has thus rekindled the need for stronger implementation of privacy-preserving AI particularly in cloud environment where privacy is a major issue. A library called TensorFlow Privacy by Google incorporates differential privacy approaches in the training process of machine learning models, while simultaneously guaranteeing data confidentiality when learning from aggregate data (Bird, 2020). This framework is proactive towards such applications like healthcare since data taken is highly sensitive as observed by Ang (2024) emphasizing that it protects patient data while training the AI model.

Likewise, PySyft created by OpenMined improves the range of federated learning by allowing data computation safely on decentralized datasets, it uses encrypted tensors and protocols such as Secure Multiple Parties Computation (Bao & Guo, 2022). The solution proposed by PySyft for federated learning deals with the weaknesses in decentralized systems pointed out by Bouacida and Mohapatra (2021).

Another fundamental concept is homomorphic encryption which forms the basis of privacy-preserving AI with organisations such as Vaultree introducing major advancements to FHE algorithms such as those demonstrated in 2024's Businesswire. Such application is emphasized by Kumar et al. (2022) to show how FHE was used to securely accumulate medical image data that can be analyzed by AI without divulging patient data.

More recent toolboxes like Crypten and TenSEAL even build upon these foundations and allow a direct integration into standard deep learning workflows (Koerner, 2023). Such tools are very helpful especially for industries that have a lot of restrictions such as the financial institutions and the healthcare industry.

PySyft however, is not the only tool OpenMined is developing; it is part of a set of tools for secure and private AI, including PyGrid, which coordinates the execution of machine learning across multiple nodes in a federated learning scheme (BW Businessworld, 2022). The incorporation of such tools helps in overcome issues in collaborative AI as discussed by Bashir et al (2024) and is also in consonance with Domingo-Ferrer and Blanco-Justicia (2020) on the use of ethical privacy preserving technologies.

Further, including the cryptographic libraries such as Microsoft SEAL and IBM HELib strengthens these frameworks, as they proposed efficient encryption techniques for secure computation (Asante et al., 2021). These libraries are significant for privacy-preserving AI in cloud systems, as noted by Acar et al. (2018) that volume showed effectiveness in the application of homomorphic encryption schemes.

Other frameworks at the application level have also materialized such as Federated learning with the modular architecture of Flower for scalable and private machine learning (Mammen, 2021). Through the integration of federated learning with differential privacy and secure aggregation, as applied by Husnoo et al. (2021), the highlighted frameworks reduce the perils related to data leakage.

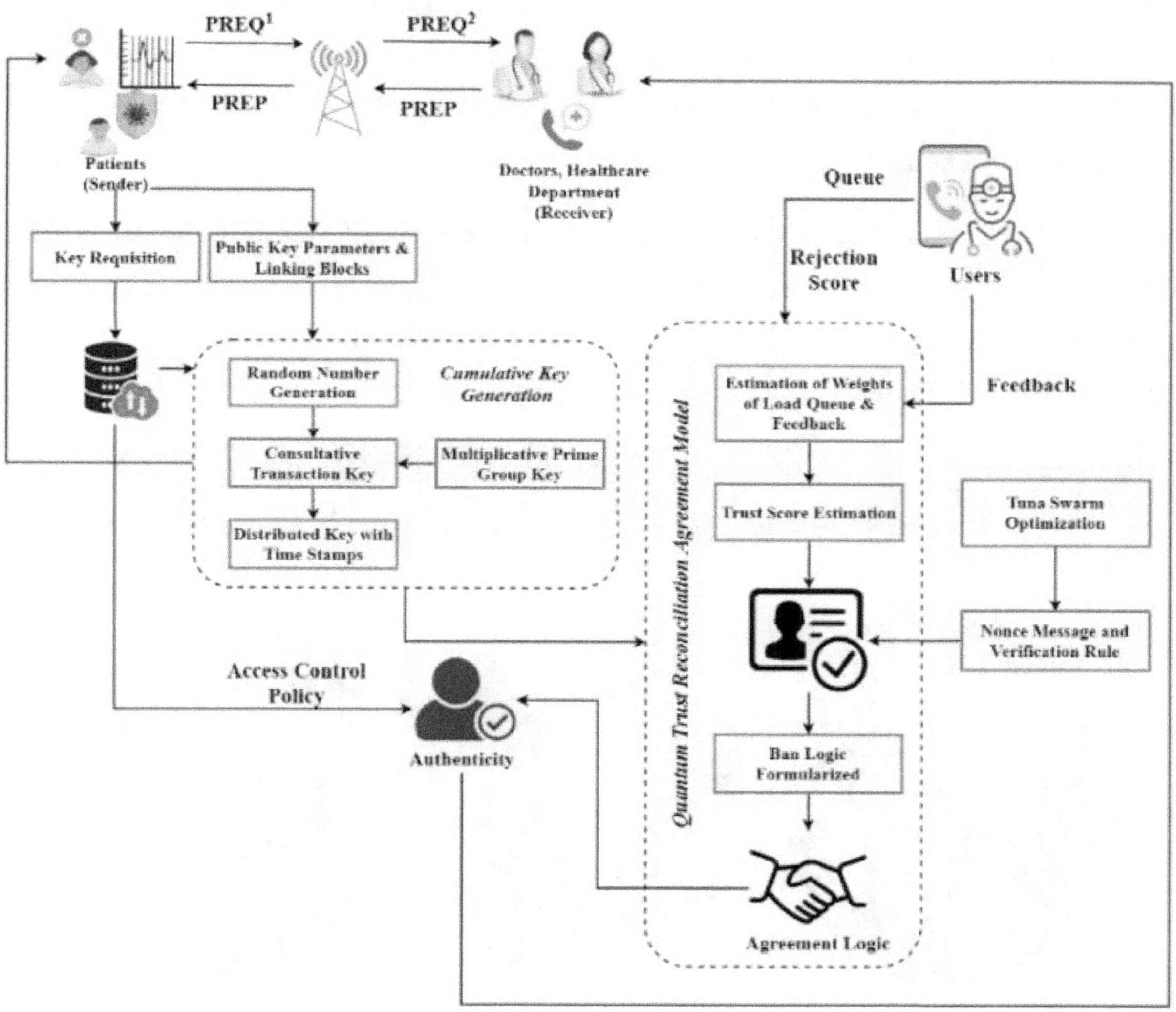

Figure 32 Blockchain cybersecurity (Nature, 2023)

Moreover, advancements such as PVML which allows for the implementation of differential privacy into data system and analytics systems are solving the problems of private AI in the enterprise setting (Lardinois, n.d.). Discussed advancements are rather useful for the resolution of the paradox perceived for AI as well as data privacy, as investigated by Michael et al. (2023).

Due to the increase in privacy with AI systems, the implementation and development of tools such as TensorFlow Privacy, PySyft, as well as, cryptographic libraries will continually play a critical role. Adherence to the strong pillars, improved encryption strategies as well as firm ethical principles provides the necessary approach to building privacy-preserving AI systems, which can respect new data protection rules and build trust in AI.

5.3 Strategies

Today, it is critical to mention that AI models in the cloud need protection based on strong and proven practices that would mitigate risks coming from various angles of data and system protection. Web services security requirements are quite similar to the requirements observed in other distributed environments; however, one of the most significant considerations is the data transfer security that allows avoiding data interception during data transfer.

Industries like Transport Layer Security (TLS) and Secure Sockets Layer (SSL) protocols offers end-user protection at the client device and cloud server and limit MITM threats. Each of these protocols of data protection have been used to secure the training datasets against some form of access or manipulation and the same applies to model parameters.

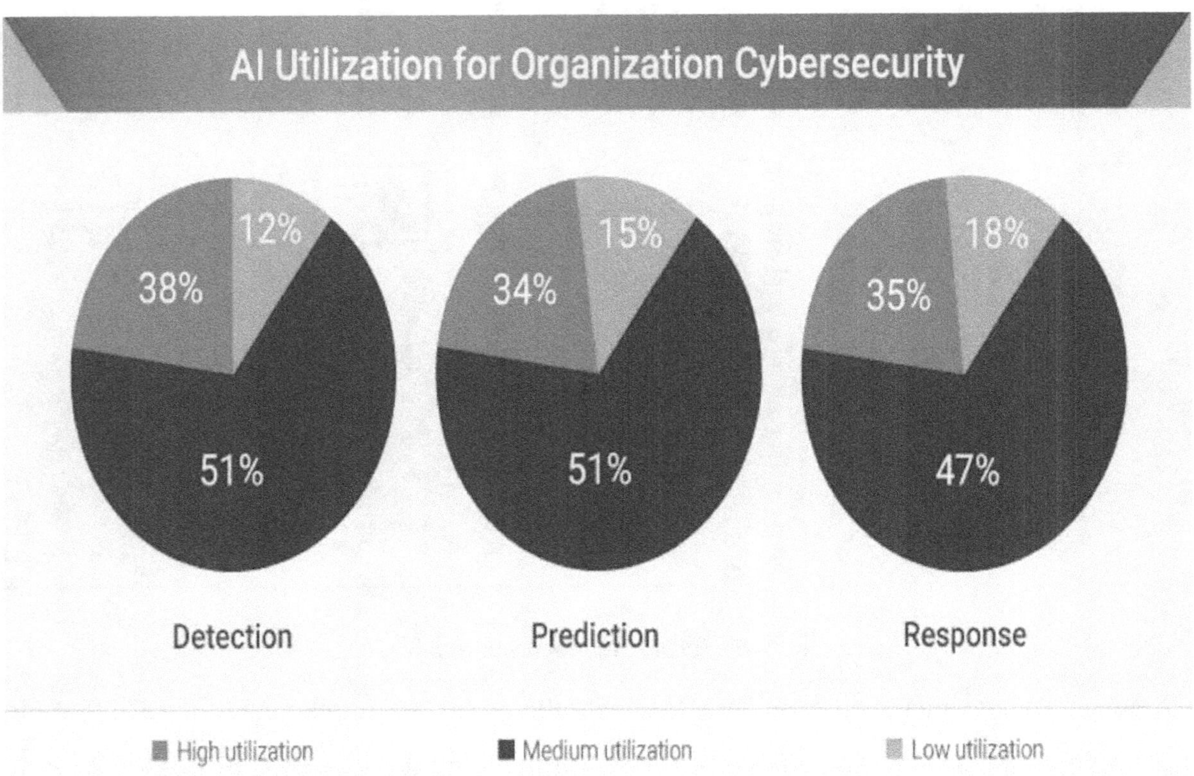

Figure 33 AI utilization in privacy issues (Bannari Amman Institute of Technology (2024)

In further security arrangements, the use of Virtual Private Networks (VPNs) and private link services can be used to create secure and isolated paths at the network layer. Also, checking adherence to ISO/IEC 27001 and SOC 2 standards provide credibility of cloud service providers, to adherent global security standards of cloud service providers for safeguarding data.

Another important strategy also entails the application of better encryption schemes as a way of protecting most AI-driven systems within clouds. Encryption makes it possible that data while it is being accessed is still in the form that cannot be understood by anyone else. Some of the cryptographic applications include: symmetric cryptography like the AES to offer data protection during storage and or transfer, asymmetric cryptography; RSA to safeguard the exchange of keys.

In addition, homomorphic encryption allow computation on encrypted data without the need of decryption in the middle so that data confidentiality could be maintained during the training or processing of AI models. This technique is particularly important when dealing with large files consisting of and a large number of records for example financial records, medical records among others.

Customer managed encryption keys (CMEKs) and Key rotation policies also have to be provided by cloud providers to provide the user more control on the encryption mechanisms. Hardware security modules (HSMs) advance the encryption tradition by protecting and creating cryptographic keys in protected environments.

That is why multi-factor authentication or MFA is another unerring factor in acting as the shield for the AI models stored in the cloud. Through the insistence on more than one method of identification, including password, a token, or biometric data, MFA limits the probabilities of imitation greatly. AWS, Azure, and Google Cloud all have MFA capabilities or have integrations with third parties that allow administrators to step up the security of AI systems.

RBAC works with MFA as a great approach to authorize only those users who require access to specific functions to perform their duties, that way restricting the menace within the organization. Administrators should also use monitoring and audit logs to track users accesses and look for any abnormal signs that require fast response to possible violations.

Another layer of reactive layer of security includes advanced security tools that include behaviour analytic and machine learning algorithms that can detect such activities as attempts at data exfiltration of large volumes of data.

To strengthen provision of cloud security to the AI models, there is the need for organizations to intensify on secure software development. It is necessary to update all the software and dependencies to handle most risks as soon as possible. Some of the practices are code signing where use of cryptographic signatures to verify that a component has not been altered by unauthorised personnel.

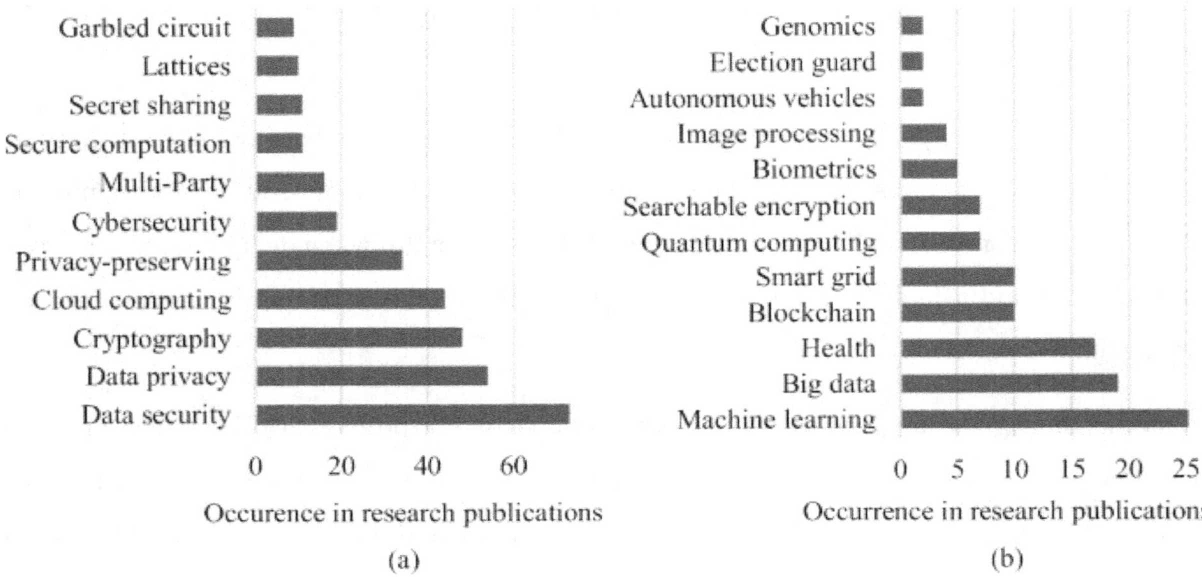

Figure 34 Privacy-Preserving neural networks (link.springer.com, 2021)

Finally, secure coding standard, vulnerability assessment, and penetration testing should be become a part of development life cycle of AI systems. Using containerisation platforms, including Docker and Kubernetes, provides enhanced layers of isolation and allow AI models to be securely enveloped and tested in isolated hydrophobic environments.

These platforms can then be extrapolated with further security policies for Network Segmentation and Resource quotas which bounds the space of attack computation. Through these strategies, the proposed approach can improve the AI system's adaptability to new threats and protect data and intellectual property and overall system's integrity.

5.4 Challenges

Deploying privacy-preserving artificial intelligence at scale requires the resolution of a set of problems, technical and organizational in the cybersecurity use case where data protection and machine learning analysis are interdependent. A first technical challenge is related to the computational cost of building privacy-preserving techniques like homomorphic encryption or SMPC.

These methods preserve the privacy of the data during processing but sometimes demand high computational power and therefore result in dilated response time and increased expenses. In response to this, organizations can use the underlying hardware accelerators including GPUs and TPUs that are most suitable for cryptographic computations.

Further, the development of lightweight encryption to secure the information involved in the model and federated learning to minimize computations' influence on the data also continue to enhance the concept. For example, using differential privacy can become the method of adding noise to the sensitive data that feeds AI models while preserving the maximum data utility.

There are available techniques that have their open-source libraries, for instance, TensorFlow Privacy, meant for applying the pointed techniques on real-world uses. The fifth is that different PPFs and cybersecurity systems are incompatible with one another challenging cross-solution consistency.

Some private components depend on the application, vendor, or configuration, so it is challenging to solve privacy issues with standardized solutions in every component. Interoperability can be changed through compliance with best practices derived from Cloud Security Alliance (CSA) standards.

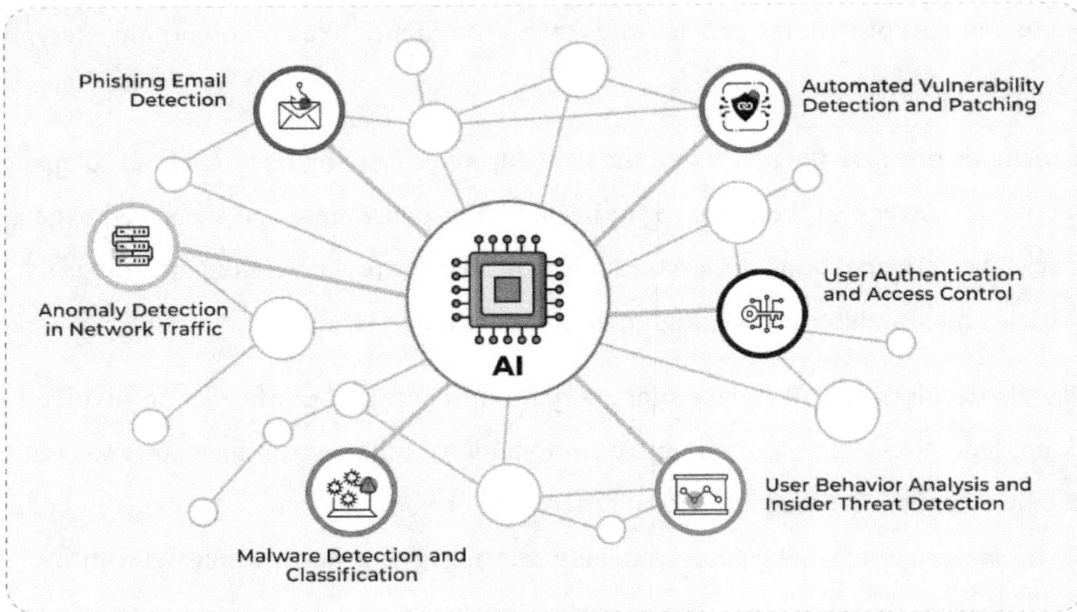

Figure 35 AI in cybersecurity (Mad Devs, 2023)

Close cooperation of AI developers, specialists in cybersecurity, and institutions regulating the industry is needed to establish the common standards that allow AI to be integrated successfully. Extensions to contemporary frameworks like container orchestration platforms like Kubernetes can serve to extend the thought process of deploying AI systems by being scalable, portable to maximize privacy.

These solutions enable organizations to share and run AI models in mixed and multiple cloud systems to function uniformly while conforming to existing operational systems. The last operational challenge is related to data quality and availability for applying privacy-preserving AI.

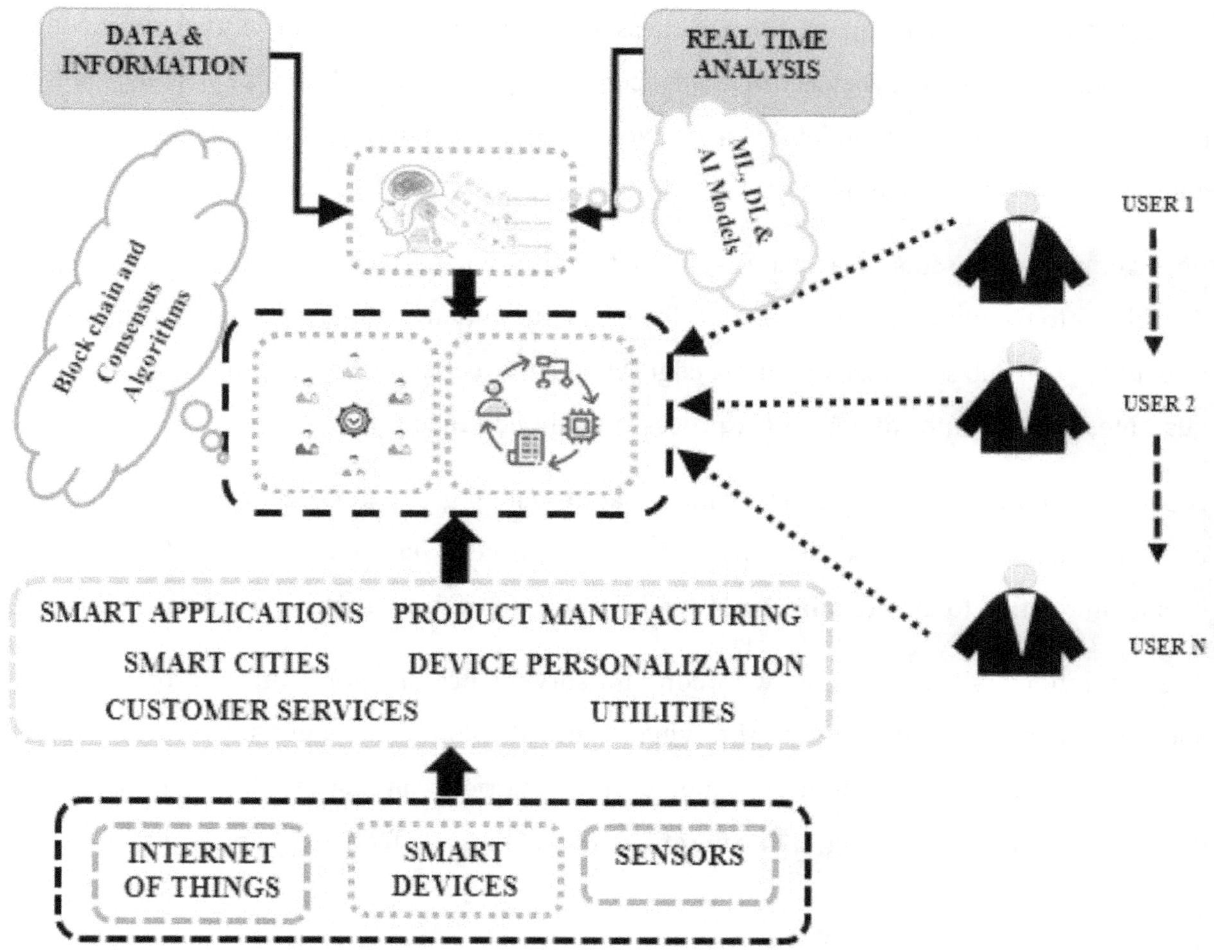

Figure 36 Blockchain based cybersecurity (Nature, 2024)

Cybersecurity applications involve the development of complex models that need a big and diverse dataset in order to learn; however, the problem of privacy hinders data sharing. This appears particularly problematic principally because of the increased focus on data privacy and protection However, synthetic data generation, which entails the generation of fake but indistinguishable datasets, may contain the solution to this issue.

Amazon SageMaker and Azure Machine Learning offer features for generating and evaluating synthetic data to allow organizations to train sound AI models without exposure of the originals. Additionally, it provides several parties the ability to train models on segmented datasets without the sharing of local data that can be highly sensitive.

The outlined approach is especially beneficial in industries where data exchange is rather limited, especially in the financial and healthcare sectors. Through the use of this method of learning, organizations get to improve their cybersecurity, and at the same time, work within legal and ethical compounds.

Another problem is related to the extensiveness of the approach, which has a direct impact on its applicability to real-life cybersecurity enhancement. Against the backdrop of growing volume and velocity of threats, AI models need to analyze huge amounts of information in real time and comply with privacy concerns.

Edge computing presents a reasonable solution for this problem since it enables the processing of data closer to the point of generation thus lowering the amount of time taken and the amount of pressure put on hub servers. Combining edge AI with the technologies that protect personal data guarantees that the information will be processed at the edge and safely.

Also, consumption of cloud service, which is auto-scaling group in AWS or scaling for Azure, using a variety of ways, it becomes possible to tailor needed resources in times of threat events in relation to the organization's available resources for optimum performance.

These solutions when integrated with constant surveillance and sometimes normal or Minor auditing make sure that privacy preserving Artificial Intelligence stays robust and effective against new threats. Through these strategies, these barriers can be overcome to transform the creation of privacy-preserving AI into the efficient, secure, and effective cybersecurity solutions.

CHAPTER 6

Future Trends

The field of privacy-preserving AI is developing fast owing to the improvement in cryptographic methods, federated learning, and PETs. Techniques like homomorphic encryption that lets computation on data in an encrypted format without decrypting them has thus come to the fore as one of the essential technologies that enable secure processing of data.

This innovation can be said to lessen the danger of leakage of data in as much as the raw data will not be within the reach of the third party or a common database or accessible to unauthorized users. Still, the problems, such as concerns over computational overhead, are still present, but corporations have been actively improving homomorphic encryption for practical usage. For instance, Microsoft SEAL and IBM HELib are samples of implementing libraries that are making the processes easier and open the door to mainstream use.

Federated learning has also received an immense response as a new approach to train AI models using data decentralization without transferring data. This approach is most useful in such sectors as the health and financial where data security is of great importance. Federated learning allows organizations to work together on developing AI while at the same respecting legal guidelines.

Google, for example offers federated learning into smart Fields employ it in medical imaging, fraud detection among other uses while NVIDIA has used in its Deep Learning working zones. In addition, new methodologies like differential privacy is being incorporated into machine learning workflows to induce mathematical privacy by making sure that an individual data point cannot be reconstructed from the results of a model.

Other novel areas, particularly those involving blockchain, are also transforming the manner of employing privacy-preserving AI. Through distributed ledgers, it becomes easier for organizations to develop records of access as well as sever processing, making it more secure and transparent.

This efficient distribution of work aligns well with blockchain, specifically with federated learning, because of its decentralized architecture that enable a secure coordination of model updates among several participants. Hence, modern PETs, such as S MPC and ZKP, are being implemented to allow for safer anonymization and data-sharing and after checks.

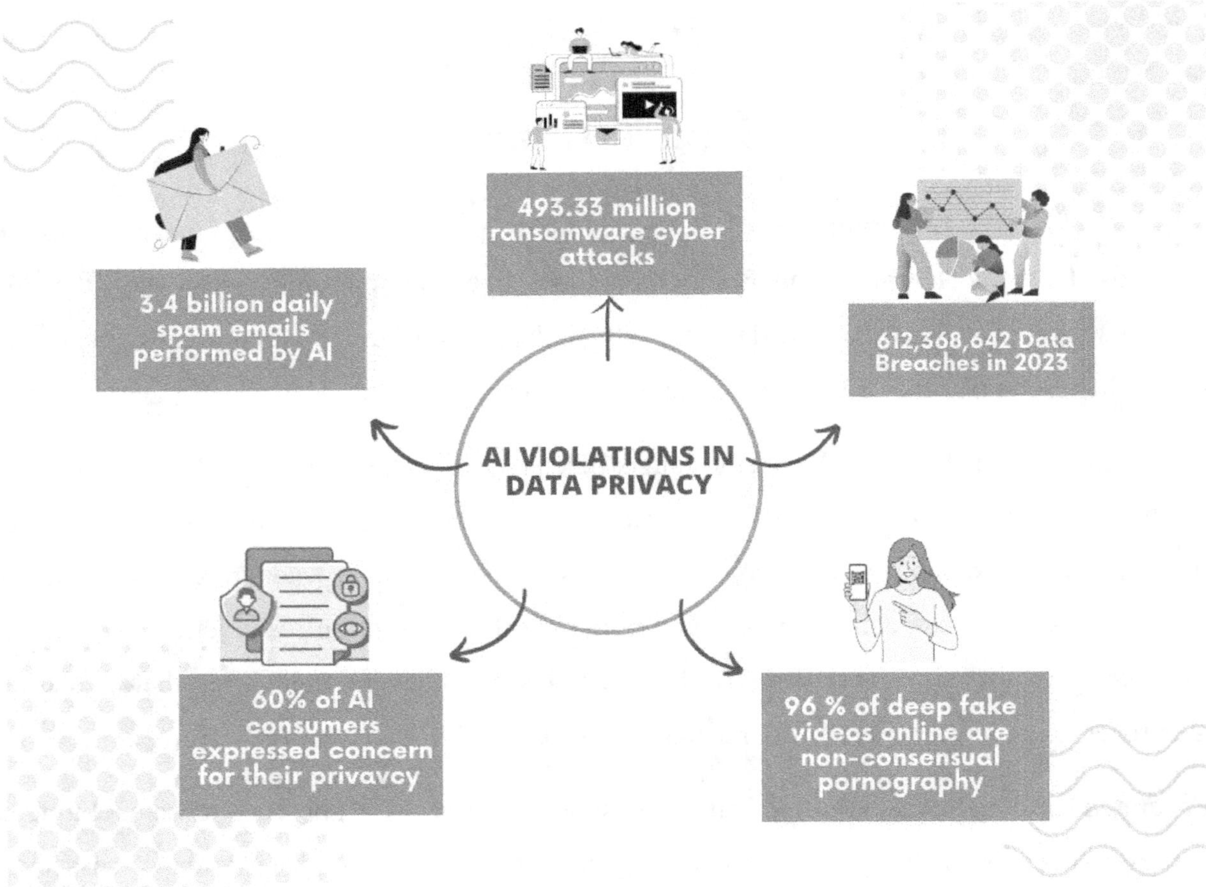

Figure 37 AI violations in data privacy (Medium, 2023)

These advancements make AI privacy an on-going working topic of research and development, that points to new breakthroughs to address issues of scalability and usability. As mentioned above, with its constant development, privacy-preserving AI technologies open a troublesome set of ethical questions such as data ownership, consent, and even the impact of using seemingly anonymous data.

Many times, organizations face a major issue of how to innovate their products while at the same time ensuring that privacy of the users is well protected. For instance, the algorithmic approaches such as differential privacy provide robust privacy, but this can bring the additional debate about the best trade-off between the privacy and the model's performance.

Ethical initiatives like the ones proposed by the European Commission regarding the use of AI incline on the characteristics of transparency as well as develop a qualitative framework towards the dealing with these matters. Observing data privacy rules another layer of complexity is introduced.

Legal norms like General Data Protection Regulation which is in force for European countries or California Consumer Privacy Act in USA provides very high standard norms for data collection, processing and data storage. It is intriguing to understand that privacy preservation in AI must also be developed to meet such regulations, some useful properties of privacypreserving AI systems include data minimization, user consent, and the right to be forgotten.

This necessity has led to a transition from compliance-based to governance-based practices and values that come with privacy by design. Other ethical challenges are also realised in the aspects of circles including bias as well as fairness. It important to note that privacy-preserving AI, like other forms of AI, can merely reiterate biases or even magnify them in the case of a biased sample dataset.

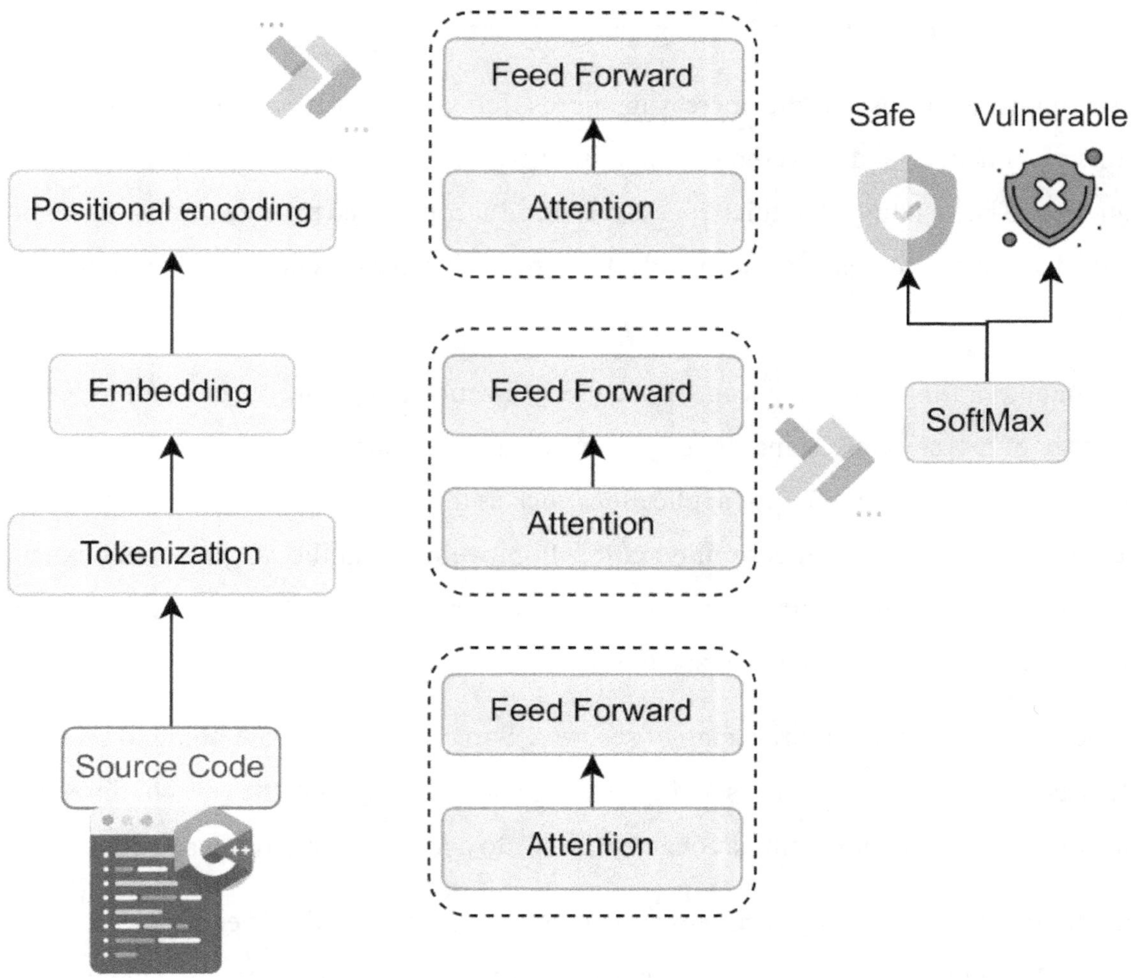

Figure 38 AI security flowchart (arXiv, 2024)

To promote fairness there must be independent testing and validation reported, and diverse representation of affected populations in the creation of AI. There is a need for so-called transparency tools, including Explainable AI (XAI) that help precisely determine the decision-making of privacy-preserving models and detect biases.

Policies related to ethical AI practices are not only a great business value, but also a great responsibility due to the increasing focus of using a privacy-centric approach. In the future, the use cases of privacy preserving AI in cloud environments will have bigger footprints, closely integrated with the cloud environment, scalable and secure.

Current cloud service providers have a fundamental responsibility in helping organizations achieve implementation of private AI and this is through providing tools and frameworks that ease the process. For instance, Google cloud's confidential computing and Microsoft Azure's confidential AI, are service models developed to protect the sensitive information input for data processing to be secure all through the computation phase.

These innovations answer the increasing needs for greater privacy in such industries as healthcare, finance, and government that is experiencing an increased adoption of cloud technology. The handling of notifications is seen to be accompanied by edge computing, which is expected to offer solutions to cloud-based AI by processing in a decentralized function closer to the sources.

When incorporating edge devices into an organization's system, organizations can take advantage of privacy-preserving AI to build systems that reduce the transfer of data to central servers. This is very important for applications such as the self-driving car and smart city where time and security are of immense importance. Improvements in the 5G Front will extend the effectiveness of edge computing and make it possible to achieve faster and secure communication between the devices and the cloud.

Other components of the future vision of secure AIS in cloud settings are going to be such factors as unity of privacy policies and governing norms. Today, specific rules in different areas present issues to any multinational that wants to adopt proper privacy standards.

More cooperation between governments, regulatory agencies, and player businesses must be achieved to set up standard more consistently encouraging innovation but also safeguard users' rights. The example of how such balance could be reached is given by the AI Ethics Guidelines by the Organisation for Economic Co-operation and Development (OECD).

The Applied Analysis section also predicts the growth of automation's involvement in privacypreserving AI, among other things. AI systems for monitoring and auditing as well as automatic updating of security and compliance of the systems will be an essential component in the complex and continually evolving cloud networks. These tools can provide means of identification of such issues, methods for enforcing accesses and even guarantee compliance to privacy regulations as applied to AI models.

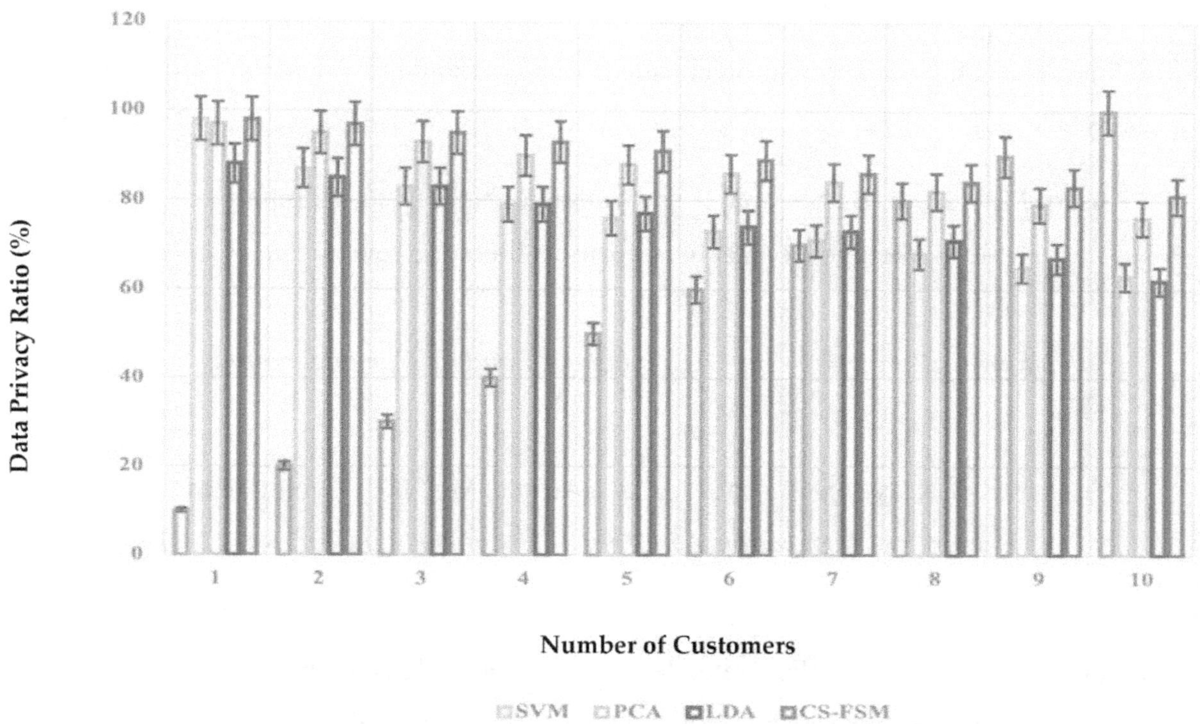

Figure 39 Impact of cybersecurity (MDPI, 2023)

Further, great expectations of quantum computing come from the fact that it is going to bring about changes in encryption that are going to secure AI systems supported on clouds with unprecedented degree. Although disruptive to the existing cryptographic standards, quantum computing is a double-edged sword since it brings the potential of designing quantum-safe AI protection techniques ahead of quantum computing breakthrough.

The development of privacy-preserving AI also shows that technology, ethics and regulation are mutually entwined. Because self-learning AI systems will increasingly feature in society, ethical frameworks and regulation will need to be sought in future. Currently, the managing organizations should step up in responding to the emerging challenges of the technical aspect while developing their AI systems and its effectiveness besides struggling to come up with ethically sound AI solutions.

REFERENCES

Acar, A., Aksu, H., Uluagac, A.S. and Conti, M., 2018. A survey on homomorphic encryption schemes: Theory and implementation. *ACM Computing Surveys (Csur)*, *51*(4), pp.1-1. https://doi.org/10.1145/3214303

Ang, A. 2024. New way to protect patient data for training AI models. *MobiHealthNews*. https://www.mobihealthnews.com/news/asia/new-way-protect-patient-data-trainingai-models

Ansari, M.F., Dash, B., Sharma, P. and Yathiraju, N., 2022. The impact and limitations of artificial intelligence in cybersecurity: a literature review. *International Journal of Advanced Research in Computer and Communication Engineering*. https://ssrn.com/abstract=4323317

Asante, G., Hayfron-Acquah, J.B. and Asante, M., 2021. Evolution of Homomorphic Encryption. *International Journal of Computer Applications*, *183*(29), pp.37-40. 10.5120/ijca2021921679

Bao, G. and Guo, P., 2022. Federated learning in cloud-edge collaborative architecture: key technologies, applications and challenges. *Journal of Cloud Computing*, *11*(1), p.94. https://doi.org/10.1186/s13677-022-00377-4

Bashir, S.R., Raza, S. and Misic, V., 2024. Progress in Privacy Protection: A Review of Privacy Preserving Techniques in Recommender Systems, Edge Computing, and Cloud Computing. https://doi.org/10.48550/arXiv.2401.11305

Bird, S. 2020, October 29. *Putting differential privacy into practice to use data responsibly.* AI For Business. https://blogs.microsoft.com/ai-for-business/differential-privacy/

Bouacida, N. and Mohapatra, P., 2021. Vulnerabilities in federated learning. *IEEE Access*, *9*, pp.63229-63249. 10.1109/ACCESS.2021.3075203

Boutin, C. 2023, December 11. *NIST offers draft guidance on evaluating a privacy protection technique for the AI ERA*. NIST. https://www.nist.gov/news-events/news/2023/12/nistoffers-draft-guidance-evaluating-privacy-protection-technique-ai-era

Businesswire. 2024. Premiering a Breakthrough in Fully Homomorphic Encryption - Vaultree Announces Next-Gen Algorithm!

https://www.businesswire.com/news/home/20240523121515/en/Premiering-aBreakthrough-in-Fully-Homomorphic-Encryption---Vaultree-Announces-Next-GenAlgorithm%21

BW Businessworld. 2022. *Ant Group makes its Privacy-Preserving computation framework open source.* https://www.businessworld.in/article/ant-group-makes-its-privacy-preserving-computation-framework-open-source-435656

Camacho, N.G., 2024. The Role of AI in Cybersecurity: Addressing Threats in the Digital Age. *Journal of Artificial Intelligence General science (JAIGS) ISSN: 3006-4023*, *3*(1), pp.143-154. https://doi.org/10.60087/jaigs.v3i1.75

Ciso, E. 2025, January 17. Donald Trump, Elon Musk discuss AI, cybersecurity with Microsoft CEO Satya Nadella. *ETCISO.in.* https://ciso.economictimes.indiatimes.com/news/cybercrime-fraud/donald-trump-elon-musk-discuss-ai-cybersecurity-with-microsoft-ceo-satya-nadella/117320273

Coker, J. 2025, January 18. Hackers use Image-Based malware and GenAI to evade email security. *Infosecurity Magazine.* https://www.infosecurity-magazine.com/news/hackers-image-malware-genai-evade/

Dalal, A. and Roy, R., 2021. CYBERSECURITY AND PRIVACY: BALANCING SECURITY AND INDIVIDUAL RIGHTS IN THE DIGITAL AGE. *JOURNAL OF BASIC SCIENCE AND ENGINEERING*, *18*(1). https://yigkx.org.cn/index.php/jbse/article/view/270

Dash, B., Sharma, P. and Ali, A., 2022. Federated learning for privacy-preserving: A review of PII data analysis in Fintech. *International Journal of Software Engineering & Applications (IJSEA)*, *13*(4). https://ssrn.com/abstract=4323967

Dilmegani, C. 2024. What is Federated Learning? Use Cases & Benefits ['25]. *AIMultiple.* https://research.aimultiple.com/federated-learning/

Domingo-Ferrer, J. and Blanco-Justicia, A., 2020. Privacy-preserving technologies. *The Ethics of Cybersecurity*, pp.279-297. https://library.oapen.org/bitstream/handle/20.500.12657/22489/1/1007696.pdf#page=287

Dumbere, D.M. and Ambhaikar, A., 2020. Application Specific Statistical Analysis of Fully Homomorphic Crypto Systems for Cybersecurity. In *Future Innovation and Sustainable Development for Asian Countries* (Vol. 83, pp. 3119-3128). The Mattingley Publishing Co., Inc. http://testmagzine.biz/index.php/testmagzine/article/view/4160

Ferrag, M.A., Friha, O., Hamouda, D., Maglaras, L. and Janicke, H., 2022. Edge-IIoTset: A new comprehensive realistic cyber security dataset of IoT and IIoT applications for centralized and federated learning. *IEEE Access*, *10*, pp.40281-40306. 10.1109/ACCESS.2022.3165809

Ferrag, M.A., Friha, O., Maglaras, L., Janicke, H. and Shu, L., 2021. Federated deep learning for cyber security in the internet of things: Concepts, applications, and experimental analysis. *IEEE Access*, *9*, pp.138509-138542. 10.1109/ACCESS.2021.3118642

Folorunso, A., Adewumi, T., Adewa, A., Okonkwo, R. and Olawumi, T.N., 2024. Impact of AI on cybersecurity and security compliance. *Global Journal of Engineering and Technology Advances*, *21*(01), pp.167-184. https://doi.org/10.30574/gjeta.2024.21.1.0193

Global, B. 2021. *Driving privacy-preserving computing technologies*. Bosch Global. https://www.bosch.com/stories/driving-privacy-preserving-computing-technologies/

Gopireddy, R.R., 2023. The Future of Cybersecurity: Innovations and Data Privacy-Preserving Techniques. *Journal of Mathematical & Computer Applications. SRC/JMCA-219. DOI: doi. org/10.47363/JMCA/2023 (2), 185*, pp.2-4. https://www.researchgate.net/profile/Ravindar-Gopireddy/publication/382857572_The_Future_of_Cybersecurity_Innovations_and_Data_Privacy-_Preserving_Techniques/links/66e43e7b2390e50b2c887d55/TheFuture-of-Cybersecurity-Innovations-and-Data-Privacy-Preserving-Techniques.pdf

Huang, J., Xu, C., Ji, Z., Xiao, S., Liu, T., Ma, N. and Zhou, Q., 2022. [Retracted] AFLPC: An Asynchronous Federated Learning Privacy-Preserving Computing Model Applied to 5G-V2X. *Security and Communication Networks*, *2022*(1), p.9334943. https://doi.org/10.1155/2022/9334943

Husnoo, M.A., Anwar, A., Chakrabortty, R.K., Doss, R. and Ryan, M.J., 2021. Differential privacy for IoT-enabled critical infrastructure: A comprehensive survey. *IEEE Access*, *9*, pp.153276-153304. 10.1109/ACCESS.2021.3124309

Johnston, L. 2020. Recent Cases Highlight Growing Conflict Between AI and Data Privacy. *Haynes Boone*. https://www.haynesboone.com/news/publications/recent-cases-highlight-growing-conflict-between-ai-and-data-privacy

Kaur, R., Gabrijelčič, D. and Klobučar, T., 2023. Artificial intelligence for cybersecurity: Literature review and future research directions. *Information Fusion*, *97*, p.101804. https://doi.org/10.1016/j.inffus.2023.101804

Khalid, M.I., Ahmed, M. and Kim, J., 2023. Enhancing data protection in dynamic consent management systems: formalizing privacy and security definitions with differential privacy, decentralization, and Zero-Knowledge proofs. *Sensors*, *23*(17), p.7604. https://doi.org/10.3390/s23177604

Khurana, R. and Kaul, D., 2019. Dynamic cybersecurity strategies for ai-enhanced ecommerce: A federated learning approach to data privacy. *Applied Research in Artificial Intelligence and Cloud Computing*, *2*(1), pp.32-43. https://www.researchgate.net/profile/Rahul-Khurana10/publication/386347451_Dynamic_Cybersecurity_Strategies_for_AI-Enhanced_eCommerce_A_Federated_Learning_Approach_to_Data_Privacy/links/67579b5334301c1fe9460d61/Dynamic-Cybersecurity-Strategies-for-AI-EnhancedeCommerce-A-Federated-Learning-Approach-to-Data-Privacy.pdf

Knodel, M., Fábrega, A., Ferrari, D., Leiken, J., Hou, B.L., Yen, D., de Alfaro, S., Cho, K. and Park, S., 2024. How To Think About End-To-End Encryption and AI: Training, Processing, Disclosure, and Consent. https://doi.org/10.48550/arXiv.2412.20231

Koerner, K. 2023. The latest in homomorphic encryption: A game-changer shaping up. *IAPP*. https://iapp.org/news/a/the-latest-in-homomorphic-encryption-a-game-changershaping-up

Kumar, R., Kumar, J., Khan, A. A., Zakria, Ali, H., Bernard, C. M., Khan, R. U., & Zeng, S. 2022. Blockchain and homomorphic encryption based privacy-preserving model aggregation for medical images. *Computerized medical imaging and graphics : the official journal of the Computerized Medical Imaging Society*, *102*, 102139. https://doi.org/10.1016/j.compmedimag.2022.102139

Lardinois, F. 2024, April 18. PVML combines an AI-centric data access and analysis platform with differential privacy. *TechCrunch*. https://techcrunch.com/2024/04/15/pvmlcombines-an-ai-centric-data-access-and-analysis-platform-with-differential-privacy/

Lauter, K. 2022. Private Artificial Intelligence: Machine Learning on Encrypted Data. *SIAM*. https://www.siam.org/publications/siam-news/articles/private-artificial-intelligencemachine-learning-on-encrypted-data/

Mammen, P.M., 2021. Federated learning: Opportunities and challenges. https://doi.org/10.48550/arXiv.2101.05428

Michael, K., Abbas, R. and Roussos, G., 2023. AI in cybersecurity: The paradox. *IEEE Transactions on Technology and Society*, *4*(2), pp.104-109. https://doi.org/10.1109/tts.2023.3280109

Miyamoto, M., Teranishi, K., Emura, K. and Kogiso, K., 2023. Cybersecurity-enhanced encrypted control system using keyed-homomorphic public key encryption. *IEEE Access*, *11*, pp.45749-45760. https://doi.org/10.1109/access.2023.3274691

Mollakuqe, E., Parduzi, A., Rexhepi, S., Dimitrova, V., Jakupi, S., Muharremi, R., Hamiti, M. and Qarkaxhija, J., 2024. Applications of Homomorphic Encryption in Secure Computation. *Open Research Europe*, *4*(158), p.158.

Munjal, K. and Bhatia, R., 2023. A systematic review of homomorphic encryption and its contributions in healthcare industry. *Complex & Intelligent Systems*, *9*(4), pp.3759-3786. https://doi.org/10.1007/s40747-022-00756-z

Nguyen, D.C., Ding, M., Pathirana, P.N., Seneviratne, A., Li, J. and Poor, H.V., 2021. Federated learning for internet of things: A comprehensive survey. *IEEE Communications Surveys & Tutorials*, *23*(3), pp.1622-1658. 10.1109/COMST.2021.3075439

Owen-Jackson, C. 2024, November 6. *What Telegram's recent policy shift means for cyber crime*. Security Intelligence. https://securityintelligence.com/articles/what-telegramsrecent-policy-shift-means-for-cyber-crime/

Poireault, K. 2025, January 18. Manchester Law Firm Leads 15,000 to Sue Google and Microsoft over AI Data. *Infosecurity Magazine*. https://www.infosecurity-magazine.com/news/law-firm-sue-google-microsoft-ai/

Rahman, A., Hossain, M.S., Muhammad, G., Kundu, D., Debnath, T., Rahman, M., Khan, M.S.I., Tiwari, P. and Band, S.S., 2023. Federated learning-based AI approaches in smart healthcare: concepts, taxonomies, challenges and open issues. *Cluster computing*, *26*(4), pp.2271-2311. https://doi.org/10.1007/s10586-022-03658-4

Schiff, A. 2020. Why Every Ad Tech Company Must Understand Differential Privacy. *Adexchanger*. https://www.adexchanger.com/privacy/why-every-ad-tech-company-must-understand-differential-privacy/

Shanmugam, L., Tillu, R. and Tomar, M., 2023. Federated learning architecture: Design, implementation, and challenges in distributed AI systems. *Journal of Knowledge Learning and Science Technology ISSN: 2959-6386 (online)*, *2*(2), pp.371-384. https://doi.org/10.60087/jklst.vol2.n2.p384

Tian, F. and Tandon, R., 2024. Inference Privacy: Properties and Mechanisms. https://doi.org/10.48550/arXiv.2411.18746

Wen, J., Zhang, Z., Lan, Y., Cui, Z., Cai, J. and Zhang, W., 2023. A survey on federated learning: challenges and applications. *International Journal of Machine Learning and Cybernetics*, *14*(2), pp.513-535. https://doi.org/10.1007/s13042-022-01647-y

Wu, N., Farokhi, F., Smith, D. and Kaafar, M.A., 2020, May. The value of collaboration in convex machine learning with differential privacy. In *2020 IEEE Symposium on Security and Privacy (SP)* (pp. 304-317). IEEE. 10.1109/SP40000.2020.00025

Wylde, V., Rawindaran, N., Lawrence, J., Balasubramanian, R., Prakash, E., Jayal, A., Khan, I., Hewage, C. and Platts, J., 2022. Cybersecurity, data privacy and blockchain: A review. *SN computer science*, *3*(2), p.127. https://doi.org/10.1007/s42979-022-01020-4

Yaacoub, J.P.A., Noura, H.N. and Salman, O., 2023. Security of federated learning with IoT systems: Issues, limitations, challenges, and solutions. *Internet of Things and CyberPhysical Systems*, *3*, pp.155-179. https://doi.org/10.1016/j.iotcps.2023.04.001

Zhang, J., Zhu, H., Wang, F., Zhao, J., Xu, Q. and Li, H., 2022. Security and privacy threats to federated learning: Issues, methods, and challenges. *Security and Communication Networks*, *2022*(1), p.2886795. https://doi.org/10.1155/2022/2886795

Zhang, L., 2024. *Differential privacy and game theory in cybersecurity* (Doctoral dissertation). http://hdl.handle.net/10453/177937

Zhao, J., Chen, Y. and Zhang, W., 2019. Differential privacy preservation in deep learning: Challenges, opportunities and solutions. *IEEE Access*, *7*, pp.48901-48911. 10.1109/ACCESS.2019.2909559

Zhu, H., Zhang, H. and Jin, Y., 2021. From federated learning to federated neural architecture search: a survey. *Complex & Intelligent Systems*, *7*(2), pp.639-657. https://doi.org/10.1007/s40747-020-00247-z

Zhu, T., Ye, D., Wang, W., Zhou, W. and Philip, S.Y., 2020. More than privacy: Applying differential privacy in key areas of artificial intelligence. *IEEE Transactions on Knowledge and Data Engineering*, *34*(6), pp.2824-2843. 10.1109/TKDE.2020.3014246

Zhu, Tianqing & Ye, Dayong & Wang, Wei & Zhou, Wanlei & Yu, Philip. 2020. More Than Privacy: Applying Differential Privacy in Key Areas of Artificial Intelligence. IEEE Transactions on Knowledge and Data Engineering. PP. 1-1. 10.1109/TKDE.2020.3014246

Ziller, A., Usynin, D., Braren, R., Makowski, M., Rueckert, D. and Kaissis, G., 2021. Medical imaging deep learning with differential privacy. *Scientific Reports*, *11*(1), p.13524. https://doi.org/10.1038/s41598-021-93030-0

www.ingramcontent.com/pod-product-compliance
Lightning Source LLC
Chambersburg PA
CBHW080217170726
48282CB00030B/1151
9789366316062